TCHOBAN VOSS
ARCHITECTS

TCHOBAN VOSS
ARCHITECTS

CONTENTS

TCHOBAN VOSS
ARCHITEKTEN

INTRODUCTION

’FACED WITH AN ARCHITECTURAL BRIEF, THE FIRST THING WE DO IS TREAT THE GIVEN URBAN SITUATION AS SOMETHING UNIQUE AND PRECIOUS. THIS IS WHERE THE ONE-OFF ARCHITECTURAL SOLUTIONS COME FROM. THE SPECIFIC URBAN CONTEXT ITSELF LEADS US TO THE RIGHT RESULT – WHICH CAN BE UNOBTRUSIVE OR STRONGLY CONTRASTING, MASSIVE OR ETHEREAL. IT IS ESSENTIAL, WE BELIEVE, TO THINK THROUGH A BUILDING FROM ITS OVERALL VOLUME DOWN TO THE DOOR HANDLES: IT IS ONLY THE INTERPLAY BETWEEN SURFACES AND INTERNAL SPACES, BETWEEN DETAILS AND THE WHOLE, THAT MAKES A BUILT STRUCTURE OR AN ARCHITECTURAL ENSEMBLE A CREDIBLE AND DISTINCTIVE PART OF ITS ENVIRONMENT.

SERGEI TCHOBAN AND EKKEHARD VOSS

The history of the architecture firm that is now TCHOBAN VOSS Architekten goes back to 1931, when it was established by the architects Sprotte and Neve. The change of name, which occurred in 2017, enshrined a change whose roots lie in the 1990s. Sergei Tchoban and Ekkehard Voss started working for what was then called Nietz Prasch Sigl Architekten in 1992. In 1995 both became partners in the firm; since 2017 they have headed it on their own. When they started out at the Hamburg office of NPS, it had a staff of 40 employees.

Today TCHOBAN VOSS Architekten has more than 150 employees from 13 countries at its offices in Hamburg, Berlin, and Dresden. Unusually for a firm of this size, staff turnover is small: employees who have been on the team for 10 or 15 years are not unusual. This is, it seems, a place where it is possible to have both a family and a career: the birth statistics for the last 10 years record 95 babies. When visiting the firm's offices, you can be sure to find a friendly, collegial, yet focused atmosphere. The two lead architects divide their responsibilities by region: Sergei Tchoban heads the Berlin office, while Ekkehard Voss is in charge of the branches in Hamburg and Dresden. They are supported by nine associates and project partners (Philipp Bauer, Axel Binder, Frank Focke, Christoph Klüsserath, Martin Krebes, Stephan Lohre, Jörg Rudloff, Dierk Schafmeyer, and Frederik-S. Scholz) and a commercial director (Jörg Schulte).

TCHOBAN VOSS Architekten's projects are as diverse as the spaces in which these buildings either fit harmoniously or emerge as landmarks, adding to what already exists or creating something new to identify with. For Sergei Tchoban and Ekkehard Voss treating the overall urban situation of an architectural brief as "something unique and precious" and taking account of both its dynamics and responsibility to the client consistently leads to a differentiated style, one which formulates a "one-off architectonic solution" in each case. The intensity with which the two partners manage individual projects is remarkable.

When you approach a building by TCHOBAN VOSS Architekten, there is always a moment of surprise: depending on the brief and the surroundings, the building may be expressive or reticent, poetic or pragmatic, loud or quiet. The projects selected for this book represent the entire range of TCHOBAN VOSS Architekten's work, in which we can see simultaneously

’ IN A WORLD THAT IS INCREASINGLY VOLATILE ONLY ARCHITECTURE THAT IS STABLE CAN SATISFY SOCIETY'S CONSTANTLY CHANGING DEMANDS. IF THE ARCHITECTURE IS EXECUTED IN A MEANINGUL AESTHETIC, AND IN A USER-FRIENDLY MANNER, IT CAN AGE GRACEFULLY AND CONTRIBUTE TO AN AUTHENTIC, LIVABLE LANDSCAPE. TO ATTAIN THIS GOAL, WE AIM FOR SOLUTIONS THAT ARE INNOVATIVE AND PRECISE AT EVERY STEP OF THE DESIGN AND CONSTRUCTION PROCESS.

SERGEI TCHOBAN AND EKKEHARD VOSS

a self-assured and narrative-oriented architectural language, an eye for details, materials, and surfaces, and a joy in preserving and in taking things forward. Our focus in this book is not just on the brand new, but also on buildings that have already proved themselves.

It was important for the architects to see their work through the eyes of others. This can be seen in the guest contributions from journalists and photographers and in the overall conceptual approach that was developed with EINSATEAM. On the following pages you will find TCHOBAN VOSS Architekten's portfolio presented in four different formats. For the eight project essays we selected buildings that illustrate the firm's aspiration of creating "unique architectural solutions"; these range from Federation Complex in Moscow City through the academic landscape of Rhine-Waal University of Applied Sciences and the sensitive renovation of the Regional Court Building in Halle to the social project for reconstructing Nauen Town Baths. Our focus stories concentrate on particular aspects of design, contrasting projects such as the Monastery Church of St. Georg - a little gem - with urbane, residential architecture, such as Living Levels or Germany's first passive pool building in Lünen.

In our thematic features, four authors look at TCHOBAN VOSS Architekten's current areas of specialization. These include housing and working environments and commercial spaces. The firm also has a wealth of experience in hotel construction and in development of existing buildings.

Finally, two reports take our readers on a visit to Bethanien-Höfe (Bethany Courtyards), an assisted-living facility and retirement home for elderly people in Hamburg-Eppendorf, and on a walk along the Spree in Berlin. The texts are illustrated with photographs by Holger Talinski; these immerse the reader in the life that has developed in and around the buildings, while letting residents and users have their say as well. The focus is on what remains - what anchors the architecture in the overall structure of an urban environment or everyday use and what allows it to function and have its effect.

Our warm thanks go to Sergei Tchoban and Ekkehard Voss, as well as to all the firm's employees who were involved, especially to Lev Chestakov, Polina Goldberg, Valeria Kashirina, and Axel Neubauer, for the insight we gained into the work of TCHOBAN VOSS Architekten during our on-site visits to the projects, in countless conversations, and during collaboration on the present publication. ■

Franziska Eidner and Jeannette Merker, EINSATEAM

BERLIN

DRESDEN

BERLIN

TODAY TCHOBAN VOSS ARCHITEKTEN HAS OVER 150 EMPLOYEES AT THREE OFFICES IN HAMBURG, BERLIN, AND DRESDEN.

PROJECT ESSAYS

What makes for a "unique architectural solution"? TCHOBAN VOSS Architekten always develop their solutions from the "overall context," i.e. the specific urban situation and the brief.

Specific approaches to a solution are demonstrated by eight projects showing how a building can benefit an entire city; how design language can serve as an element on which to build identity; how lost beauty can shine anew; how a functional building can become an architectural landmark; and how a design approach may be reflected in the smallest details.

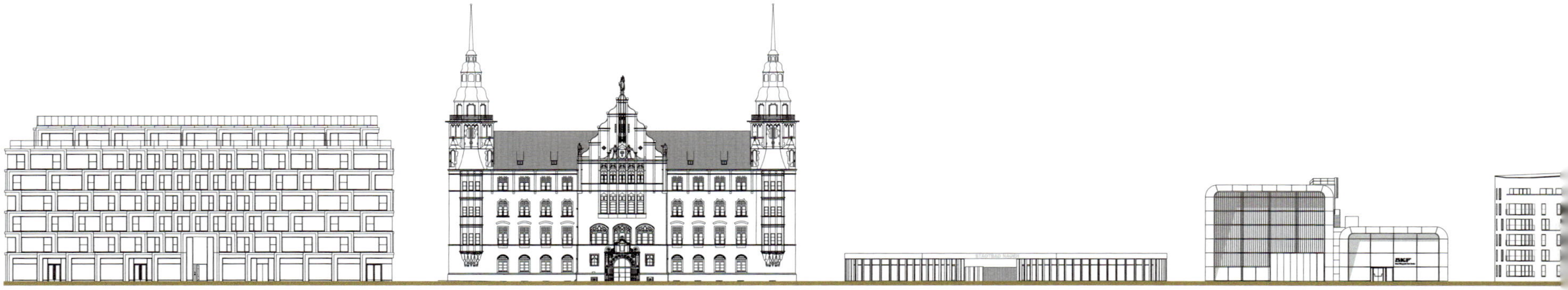

MUSEUM FOR
ARCHITECTURAL DRAWING, BERLIN

LANDGERICHT HALLE

NAUEN TOWN BATHS

FEDERATION COMPLEX, MOSCOW

HOUSING ON
HOLZHALBINSEL, ROSTOCK

BOXHAGENER STRASSE, BERLIN

RHINE-WAAL UNIVERSITY
OF APPLIED SCIENCES, KLEVE

SVEN WINGQUIST
TEST CENTER, SCHWEINFURT

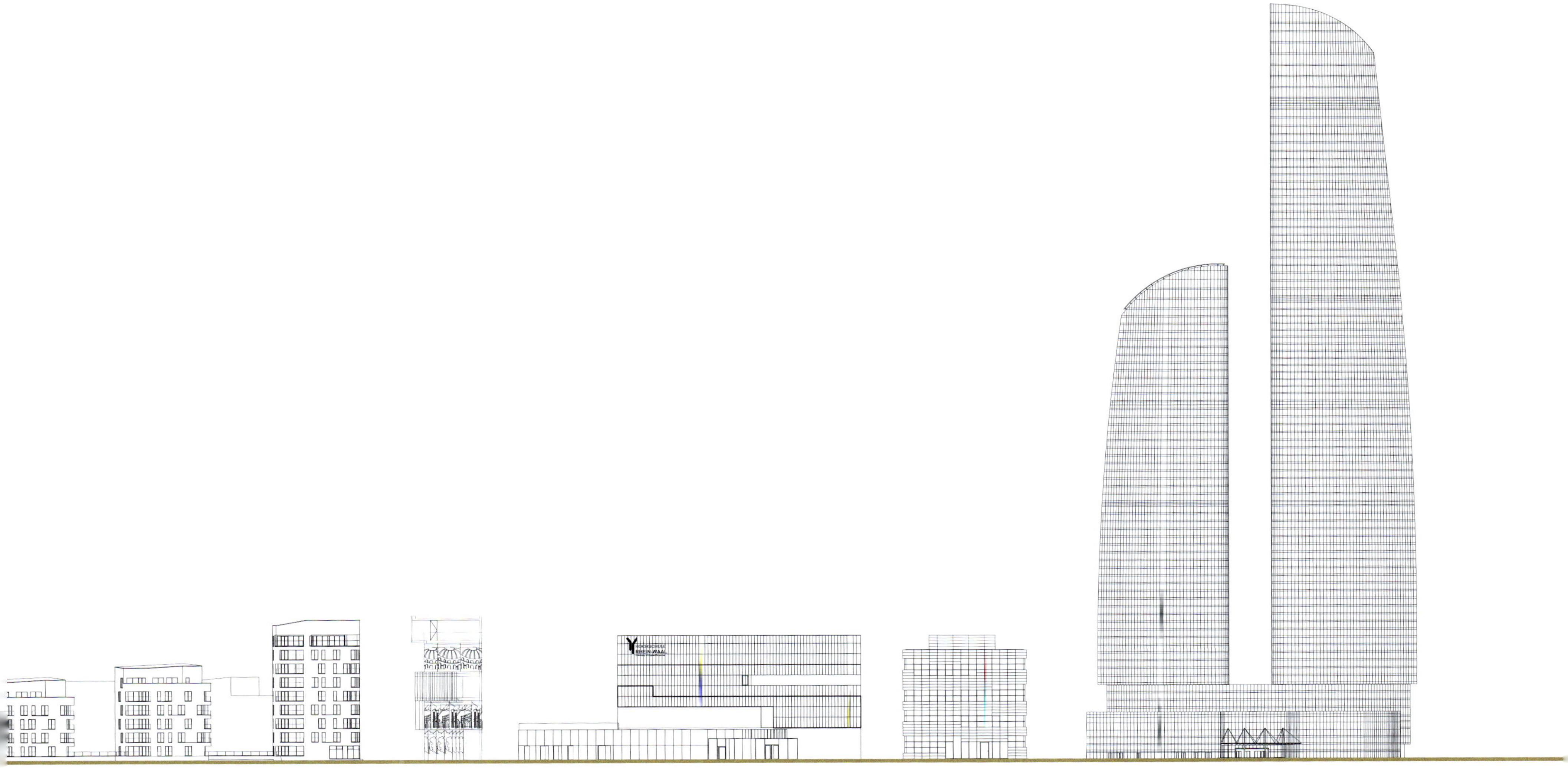

EMBLEMATIC: A BUILDING AS GESAMTKUNSTWERK

MUSEUM FOR ARCHITECTURAL DRAWING

’ BEAUTIFULLY BUILT AND PRECISELY DETAILED, IT HAS THE CHARACTER OF A MODERN GESAMTKUNSTWERK.

CATHERINE SLESSOR,
ARCHITECTURAL REVIEW

If the architect is both designer and client, then it can be assumed that here is a work of architecture that uncompromisingly reflects the values and attitudes of its creator. In the Museum for Architectural Drawing in Berlin this assumption is confirmed down to the last detail. Described by Architectural Review as a "modern gesamtkunstwerk," and specializing, uniquely for Germany, in freehand architectural drawing, this museum building has enriched Berlin's exhibition landscape since 2013.

Sergei Tchoban's objective was to create a venue offering ideal conditions for exhibiting and storing graphic works of art. The architectural design was developed by Tchoban in collaboration with Sergey Kuznetsov, his former partner at his Moscow architecture firm SPEECH. Subsequent planning of the building was taken over by TCHOBAN VOSS Architekten. The result is an "emblematic building" (Berliner Morgenpost), which shows "rigorously and exquisitely at the same time … what its function and its content are" (Frankfurter Allgemeine Zeitung). But this is not just a venue offering ideal conditions for exhibiting and archiving architectural drawings; it is also a building that even on the outside conveys with a grand narrative gesture what it contains within.

Situated at the edge of what used to be the grounds of the Am Pfefferberg brewery, whose cultural and gastronomic options, workshops, and ateliers make it an important crystallization point in Berlin's current creative scene, the new museum is an autonomous statement of contemporary architecture. The architects have stacked four storeys on top of, and offset against, one another. Crowning the building is a glazed cube with terraces, which opens up a clear view of the Pfefferberg area to the east and of the surrounding residential neighborhood around Teutoburger Platz to the west. A central principle of TCHOBAN VOSS Architekten is to involve the urban context, making intelligent use of it as the basis for new architectural design, which is precisely what we have here. The narrative motif of stacked archive boxes (of the kind that have diverse applications in museums) and the detailed and expressive design of the façades represent fundamental values for the architects, as does the care taken in the execution and choice of materials.

In reference to the building's function and content, the sand-colored concrete façade displays large-format fragments of historical architectural drawings, made on site using formwork. On the ground floor and all the way up the staircase are small windows of cathedral glass cut into the concrete on the courtyard side; these break up the façade illustration structurally. On the building's envelope there unfolds, says Sergei Tchoban, "an interplay between fine, dynamic, occasionally fragile drawing and expansive, robust construction."

’RIGOROUSLY AND EXQUISITELY AT THE SAME TIME, THIS BUILDING SHOWS WHAT ITS FUNCTION AND CONTENT ARE.

GERWIN ZOHLEN, FRANKFURTER ALLGEMEINE ZEITUNG

The building can be entered from both the Pfefferberg grounds and from the street. Two large apertures are formed by recesses: one is an entrance niche; the other, a glazed loggia. The functions of the interior space are clearly structured, follow the vertical division, and correspond to the particular spatial and technical needs involved in their specific uses. The ground floor contains the entrance and ticket office. The exhibition spaces are on the first and second floors. The archive, with an extensive collection of approximately 2500 pieces, including works by Oscar Niemeyer, Zaha Hadid, and Lebbeus Woods, is on the third floor. Above it is the office and meeting area with the glazed envelope and terrace.

“Just as an architectural draughtsman develops his drawing down to the smallest detail,” observes Sergei Tchoban, “so the museum came into being down to the doorknob, all of one piece, as a work of design.” This consistent, coherent approach to design can be seen in every angle and line in the treatment of both the building's interior and exterior. The new museum’s eloquent and yet highly functional architecture has received considerable international recognition, including numerous prizes and nominations. ■

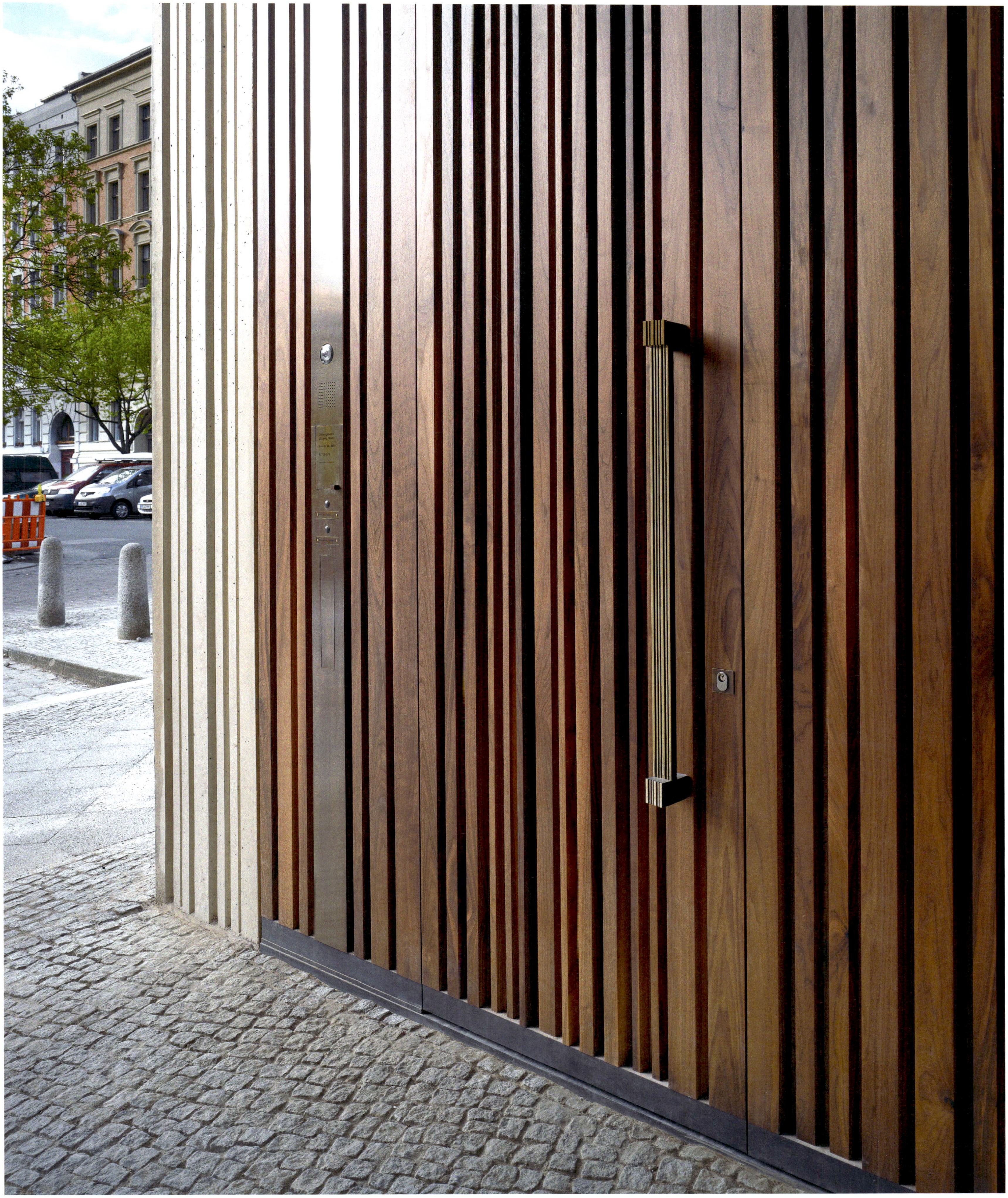

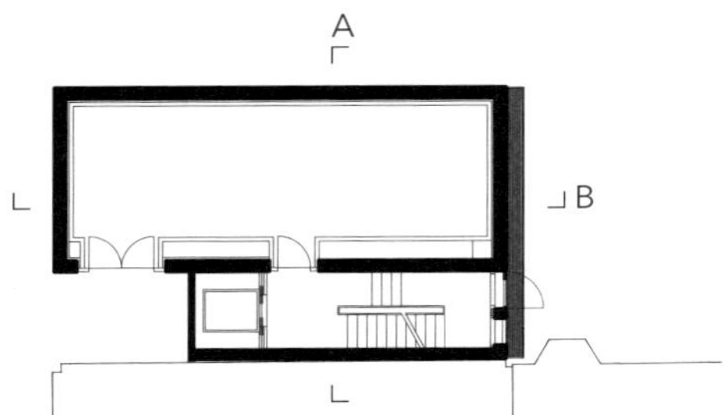

FLOOR PLAN.
GROUND LEVEL

FLOOR PLAN.
LEVEL 1

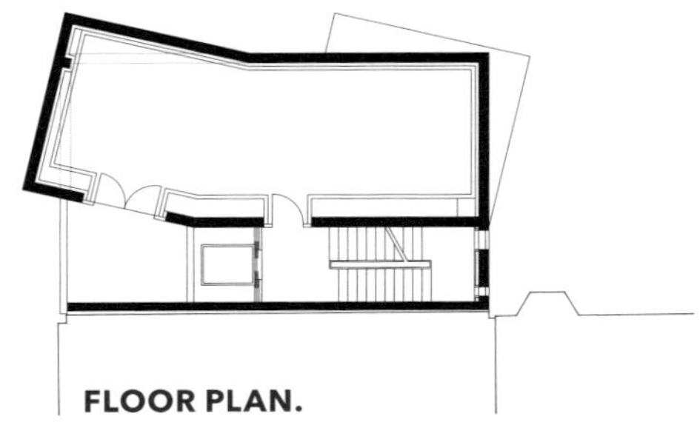

FLOOR PLAN.
LEVEL 2

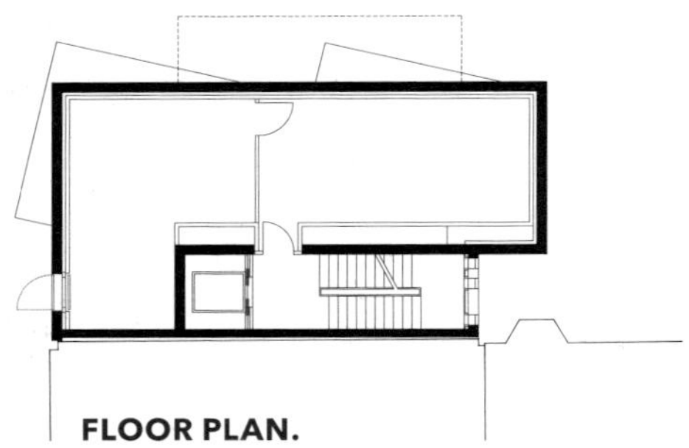

FLOOR PLAN.
LEVEL 3

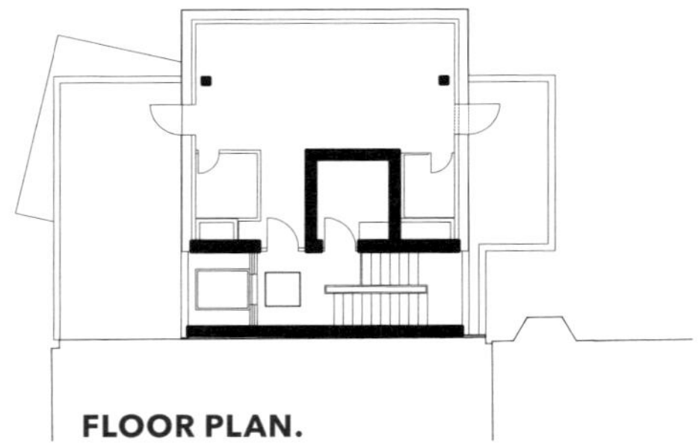

FLOOR PLAN.
PENTHOUSE

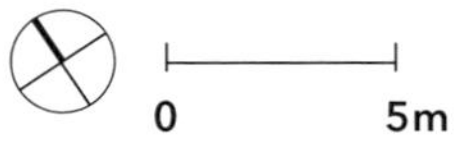

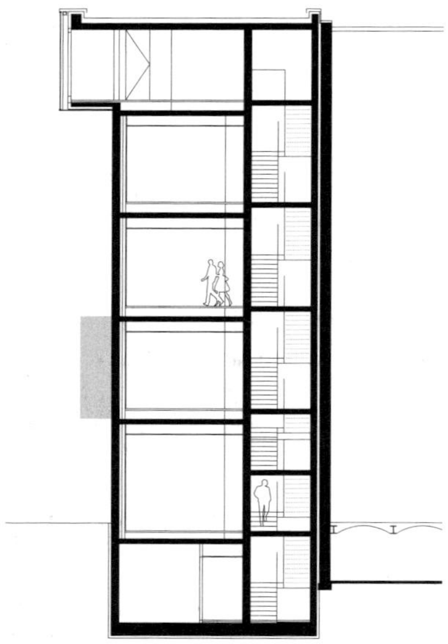

SECTION AA

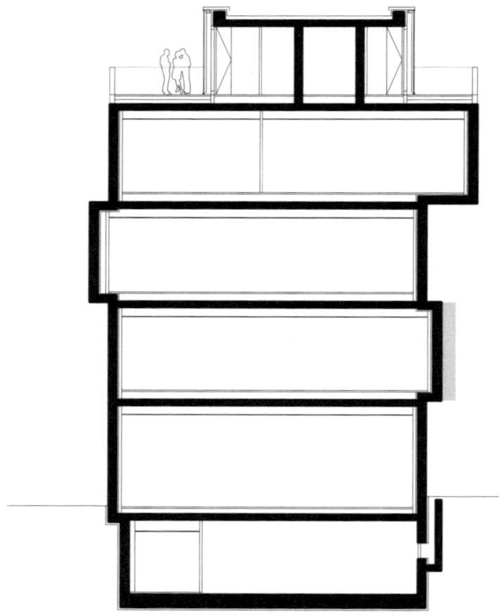

SECTION BB

A JEWEL FOR THE JUDICIARY: OLD BEAUTY BURNISHED FOR MODERN USE

LANDGERICHT HALLE

’ **THE OLD BEAUTY NOW SHINES AGAIN.** YOU ONLY HAVE TO LOOK AROUND YOU TO HAVE NO DOUBT THAT IN THIS THE JUDICIARY HAS GAINED A REAL JEWEL.

PROFESSOR ANGELA KOLB-JANSSEN,
MINISTER FOR JUSTICE FOR SACHSEN-ANHALT

Fire-safety, up-to-date communications equipment, and the need to eliminate building defects were the practical considerations that in 2011 led to the decision to renovate the regional courthouse in Halle. Additionally, the Sachsen-Anhalt region, as client, wanted to bring to light the original beauty of this "palace of justice," that was erected in 1905 as a courthouse and has been used as such ever since. The refurbishing contract given to TCHOBAN VOSS Architekten was therefore, from the beginning, also a matter of meticulous care for this listed building.

The regional courthouse in the east of the historical center of Halle (Saale) is one of the most representative buildings in the city. This architectural monument with its Neo-Baroque, double-towered façade and abundance of decorative elements that cite the Gothic and Early-Renaissance styles, is one of the most important court buildings of the Wilhelmine period. Due to its continuous use over the course of more than 100 years and structural neglect over the same period of time, its internal appearance in particular had long since ceased to live up to its representative function. Traces of time and of use were inscribed in the building - moisture damage on the ceilings, noticeable signs of wear and weathering, and overpainting from previous renovations. The renovation project needed to recreate in all of its opulence the building's condition at the time of its construction, while upgrading the facilities to meet today's standards for security and working conditions. In addition to restoring the façades, the renovation and refurbishment encompassed 20 courtrooms, 110 offices, and 103 other rooms, including the library, the archives room, presentation spaces, and technical spaces, such as corridors and staircases. The meticulous reconstruction of the building's original condition focused in particular upon the entrance area and its imposing main staircase. Here TCHOBAN VOSS Architekten worked together with restorers and specialized craftsmen. The project manager coordinated up to 50 companies who were working at the same time.

Preliminary restoration studies showed that the staircase, with its 442-meter-high domed hall and impressive, reticulated vaulting, as well as some of the corridors and rooms, were originally of a much more splendid design than suggested by the plain color scheme before renovation work began. Since uncovering and retouching the original paintwork was not possible for reasons of cost, it was reconstructed instead. The splendid floral elements and colorful patterns now allow the rooms to shine with a new opulence. A special highlight is the banisters of the spiral staircase. In place of the previous wine-red color, there are now light-green leaves and gold blossoms spreading up the staircase. Particular attention was also paid to the original six courtrooms, whose authentic furnishings were for the most part still in existence. The negotiation rooms each had their own different color scheme and décor.

The refurbishment and reconstruction proceeded with great sensitivity, extending to details such as the multi-layered wall stencils, door frames, door panels, lead glazing, wooden panelling, and fittings - which come together to constitute a coherent picture, doing justice to this building's importance and function. In the same category are the state-of-the-art additions, such as the glazed fire-safety doors and the integration of elaborate communications and security equipment, including sensitive additions like functional furniture and lighting. "In this renovation of one of the most architecturally important courthouses in Prussia," says the building and real-estate management department for Sachsen-Anhalt, the client for this far-reaching commission, "we managed to meet the highest requirements for the care of a listed building while fitting it out with state-of-the-art equipment." ■

HALLE
MERSEBURG
BITTERFELD

> ’THE LIGHT THAT THIS BUILDING NOW POSSESSES SYMBOLICALLY SHOWS THAT JUSTICE IS OPEN TO ALL AND IS THERE FOR CITIZENS. THE REGIONAL COURT IS A GEM FOR HALLE AND THE SACHSEN-ANHALT REGION.

PROFESSOR ANGELA KOLB-JANSSEN,
MINISTER FOR JUSTICE FOR
SACHSEN-ANHALT

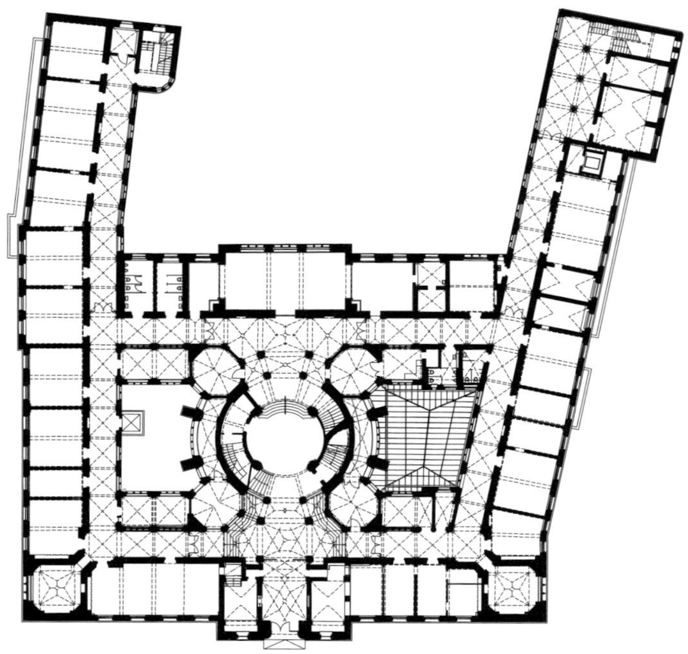

FLOOR PLAN. GROUND LEVEL

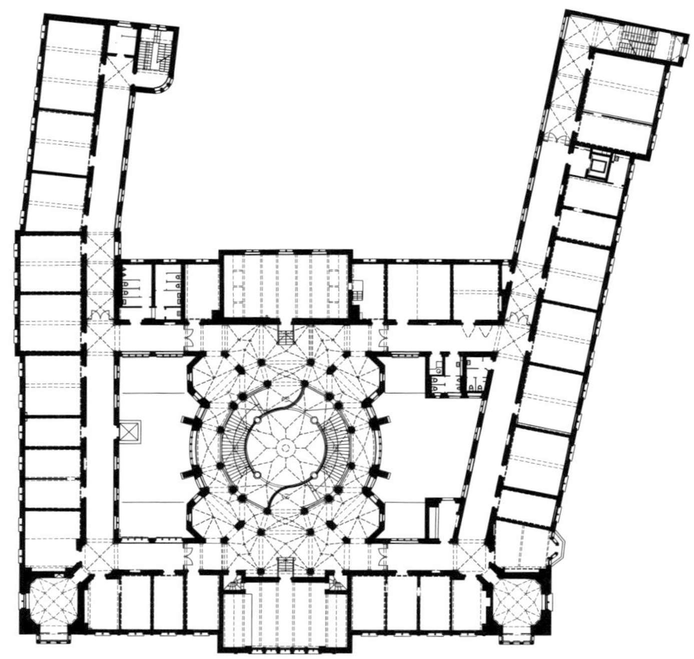

FLOOR PLAN. LEVEL 3

0 10 m

19
04
ERSTE ZIVIL-KAMMER
78

FROM OPEN-AIR POOL TO MULTIFUNCTIONAL MEETING PLACE

NAUEN TOWN BATHS

‚THE RECONSTRUCTION OF THE POOL IS A KEY PROJECT IN THE TOWN'S SOCIAL PROGRAM.

DETLEF FLEISCHMANN,
MAYOR OF NAUEN

The intention of the federal/regional "Social City" program is to upgrade city neighborhoods not just in terms of urban planning, but also with a view to sustainably improving inhabitants' living conditions and to reinforcing their identification with city districts. How this can be achieved is shown by the construction, funded by this program, of an entrance building for Nauen town pool. What has been created is an all-year-round place for leisure as well as a meeting place for all inhabitants of Nauen.

The new structure opened in August 2017, after barely a year of construction. The project was preceded by a citizens' participation process and an architectural competition, won by TCHOBAN VOSS Architekten. The jury was won over by the planners' "effective distribution of functions," which put the summer and year-round operation of the pool in two interconnected, but separately usable blocks. The two pavilion-like buildings unfold like buds, their shapes fitting well into their natural surroundings and making it possible to reduce energy consumption for the all-year operation of the new café, district management's advice center, and wellness center.

The approximately 2.6-hectare site is situated south-east of the historical city center in an area of comparatively sober residential development. The Karl-Bernau-Ring/Inner City East area has a population of approximately 2500. It is all of the inhabitants of Nauen, however, and not just local residents, who benefit from the pool's reconstruction and from its transformation into an urban community center.

The history of the pool goes back to 1967. The entrance building had been out-of-date for a very long time and was entirely demolished to make way for the new building. The organic shape, materiality, and the color of the two one-storey blocks harmonize with the nature-like landscaping of the baths. A striking, curving attic strip links the two buildings and creates the feeling of an entrance gateway. The roof is made from prefabricated plank elements. Wooden frames form both the load-bearing structure and the building's façade. The latter consists of prefabricated, polygonal wooden frames with double glazing and insulated wooden panels in shades of green in the enclosed façade areas. The structure was developed specially for this project in collaboration with Mohrmann Bau of Alfstedt. In addition to paying attention to the façade's design, the architects also sought to ensure that it would be as easy to clean as possible.

The southern part of the complex contains a café with a multi-use space, an advice center, and a new wellness area and sauna. All these areas are accessible separately from the forecourt and can be used independently of one another. The northern block contains spaces for use by swimmers in the summer. The layouts of the two pavilions follow an orthogonal pattern. The auxiliary spaces are concentrated in the inner core area and generous spaces have been created that lead outside, alongside the curving façades. The inviting character of the design thus continues from the inside to the outside. The outside spaces, the wellness area, and the café are open all year round: the town pool has become a meeting place. ■

STADTBAD NAUEN

’ IT NOT ONLY HELPS UPGRADE THIS RESIDENTIAL AREA, **IT BENEFITS THE ENTIRE TOWN TOO.**

DETLEF FLEISCHMANN,
MAYOR OF NAUEN

STADTBAD NAUEN

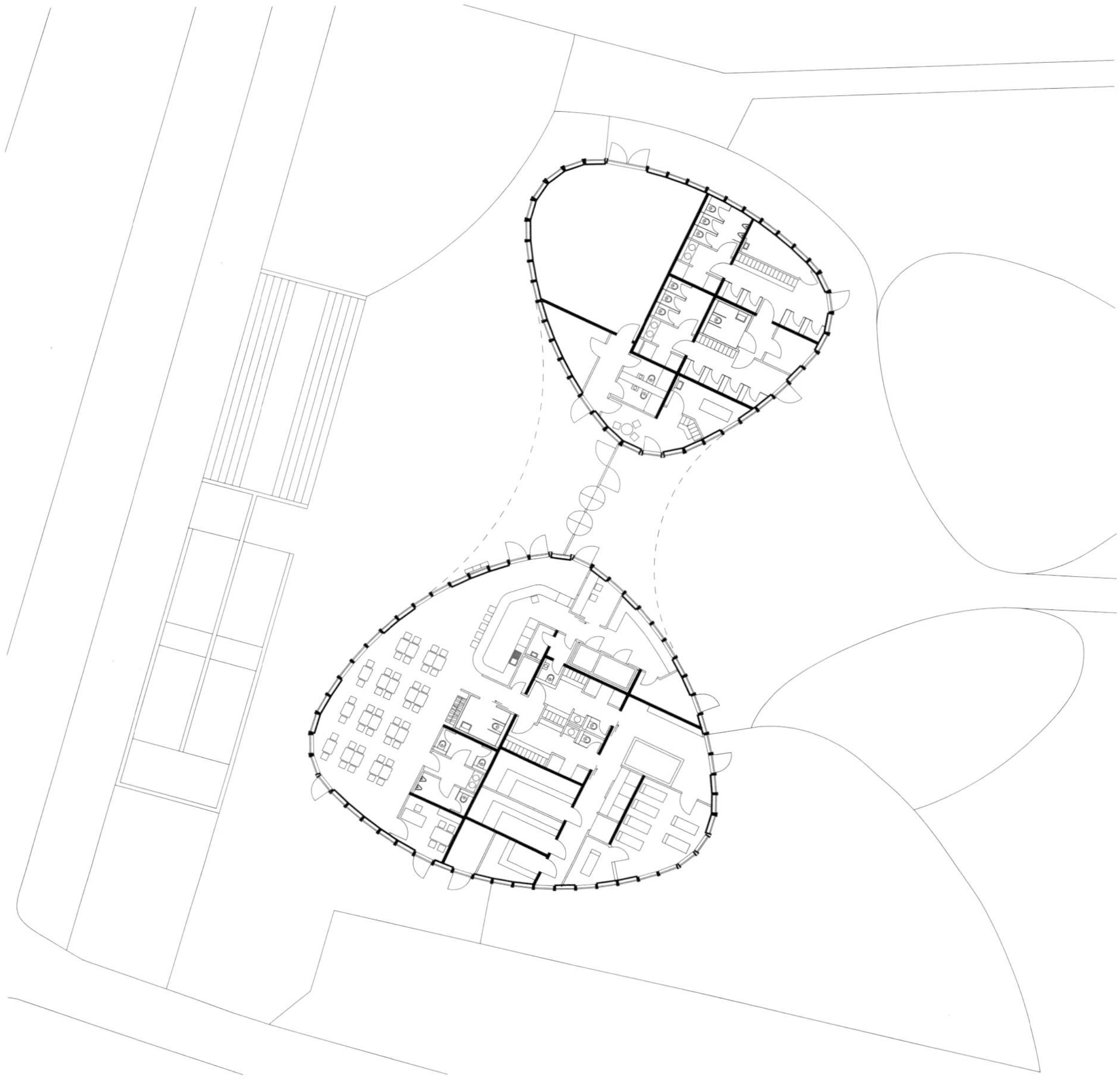

The pavilions' internal layout conforms to an orthogonal grid: the ancillary rooms are concentrated in the innermost area, while large spaces have been created along the façades.

A NEW SYMBOL FOR THE GROWING METROPOLIS

FEDERATION COMPLEX

' **THE STRIKING APPEARANCE OF THE TWO TOWERS HAS CONSPICUOUSLY CHANGED MOSCOW'S SKYLINE.** THE COMPLEX ATTRACTS BOTH BUSINESSES AND TOURISTS. SO IT'S HARDLY SURPRISING THAT THE FEDERATION IS ALREADY BEING SOLD AS A NEW LANDMARK OF MOSCOW.

URBAN-HUB.COM

The extent to which Moscow has changed over the last decade becomes clear even as you fly into the Russian capital. "Moscow City," a district on a 100-hectare site on the embankment of the River Moskva, is Moscow's new business center and growing fast. Up to 300 000 people will work here in the future. The new business district with its skyscrapers is already known as "Manhattan on the Moskva." High-rises have long been a part of Moscow's urban center, but Moscow City sets new standards. The district is rising up on what used to be wasteland in the middle of the city, bordered by the River Moskva on one side and main roads on the other. Development began in the 1970s with the International Trade Center. The early 1990s brought the first sketches of the business district as a "city within a city." Prototypes are London's Docklands or La Défense in Paris.

Consisting of two towers, the Federatsiya Complex, also known internationally as "the Federation Complex," stands right in the middle and with its 374-meter tower is the tallest building in Moscow. Upon its completion in 2017, this was even the tallest skyscraper in Europe.

It is not just its height and prominence in the structure of the city that make the Federation Complex a superlative achievement. This is the district's first mixed-use building and a consistent embodiment of the "vertical city" concept. It is also a sign of the complexity of the construction brief in which TCHOBAN VOSS Architekten played a key part for more than a decade. The result is a two-tower complex built according to a design by Sergei Tchoban and Peter Schweger. TCHOBAN VOSS Architekten and SAA Schweger Architekten took first place as a consortium in the international competition held in 2003. Realization of the project was led by TCHOBAN VOSS Architekten. Following the laying of the foundation stone in 2005, the construction process was accompanied by extensive modifications, compromises, and an economic crisis. Tower West, the smaller of the two towers, was completed in 2008; the taller Tower East was finally finished in 2017.

The quest for a shape for the Federation Complex proved long and exacting. As a new symbol of the capital, the building needed to have a very plastic, expressive, and at the same time clear design that would form an equally impressive new skyline for Moscow when seen from very different points of view in the city. The coherent design approach extends to the curved glass roof, which makes do without any of the usual technical superstructures. Additionally, the building needed to be attractive on a human scale, from the ground level, and from above, fitting within the structure of the city. This function is performed by the six-storey rectangular plinth structure that serves as the base for the dynamic composition of buildings. Its curving glass façade creates visual accents - a design element that extends vertically throughout the entire complex.

’THIS IS THE DISTRICT’S FIRST MIXED-USE BUILDING AND A CONSISTENT EMBODIMENT OF THE ‘VERTICAL CITY’ CONCEPT.

The transition between the plinth and the towers is emphasized by a four-storey waist with bridges that link Tower East and Tower West to form a coherent whole. The storeys above the podium form a layout shaped like a diagonal lens and jump back towards the towers, whose heights of 242.7 and 373.7 have a ratio of 2:3 to one another. The almost entirely glazed towers are based on the shape of two equilateral triangles, which taper upwards along a slightly outwardly-curving outline.

The 95 floors of Tower East accommodate offices, apartments, places to eat, and a fitness club. There are spectacular uses, some of them open to the public, integrated into the upper floors. The supreme efficiency with which the spaces on individual floors in the towers were designed was also due to a technical novelty: the Federation Tower was the first building in the world to be fitted with Twins – two lifts in the same shaft – by Thyssen Group. On its 63 floors Tower West has, in addition to offices and apartments, a swimming pool and restaurants. Federation Complex additionally offers spaces for retail trade, a congress center, and an underground "Lifestyle Center," with places for eating and entertainment.

The geometry of the building continues inside as well, becoming a consistent design code. For the interior of the Federation Complex, Sergei Tchoban created a variety of elements such as doorknobs, lights, and light switches. These bring the vocabulary of forms inside the building from its exterior and, down to the smallest details, serve as a distinctive symbol of the entire center. ■

CHANNEL

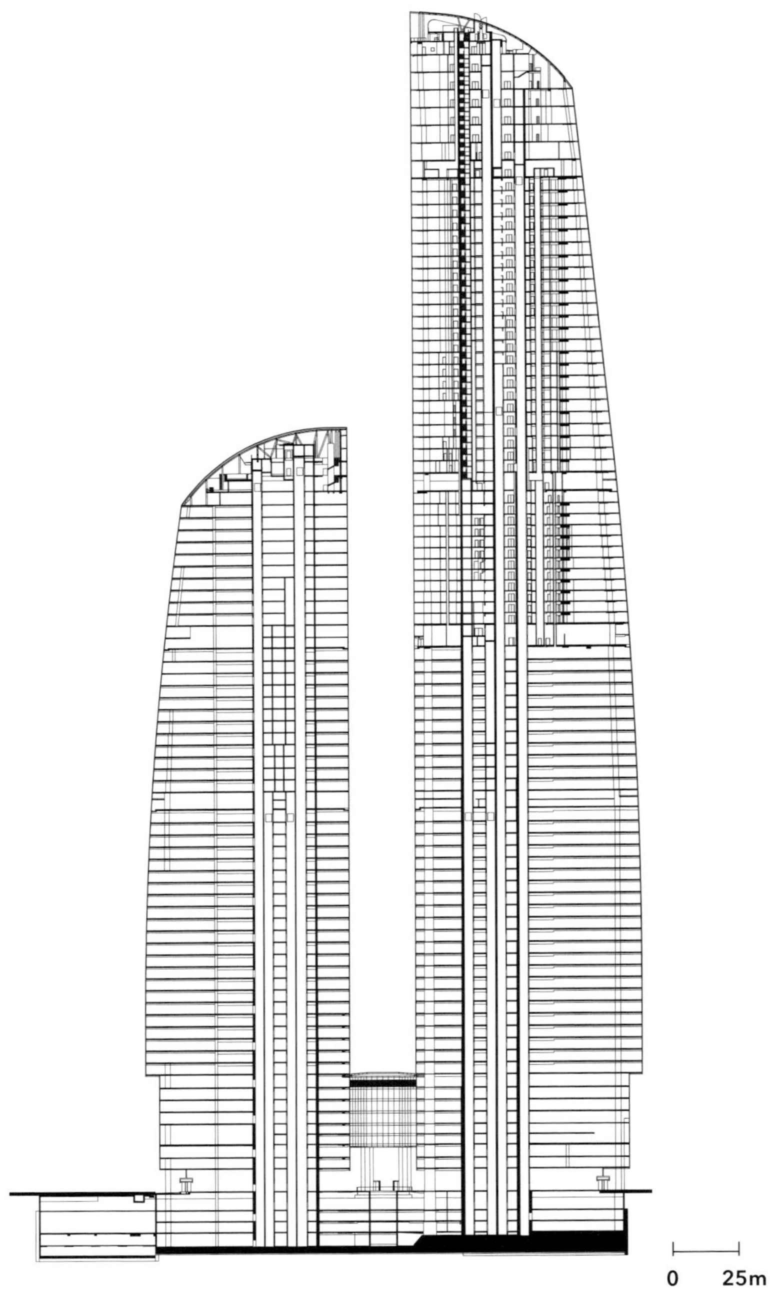
0 25m

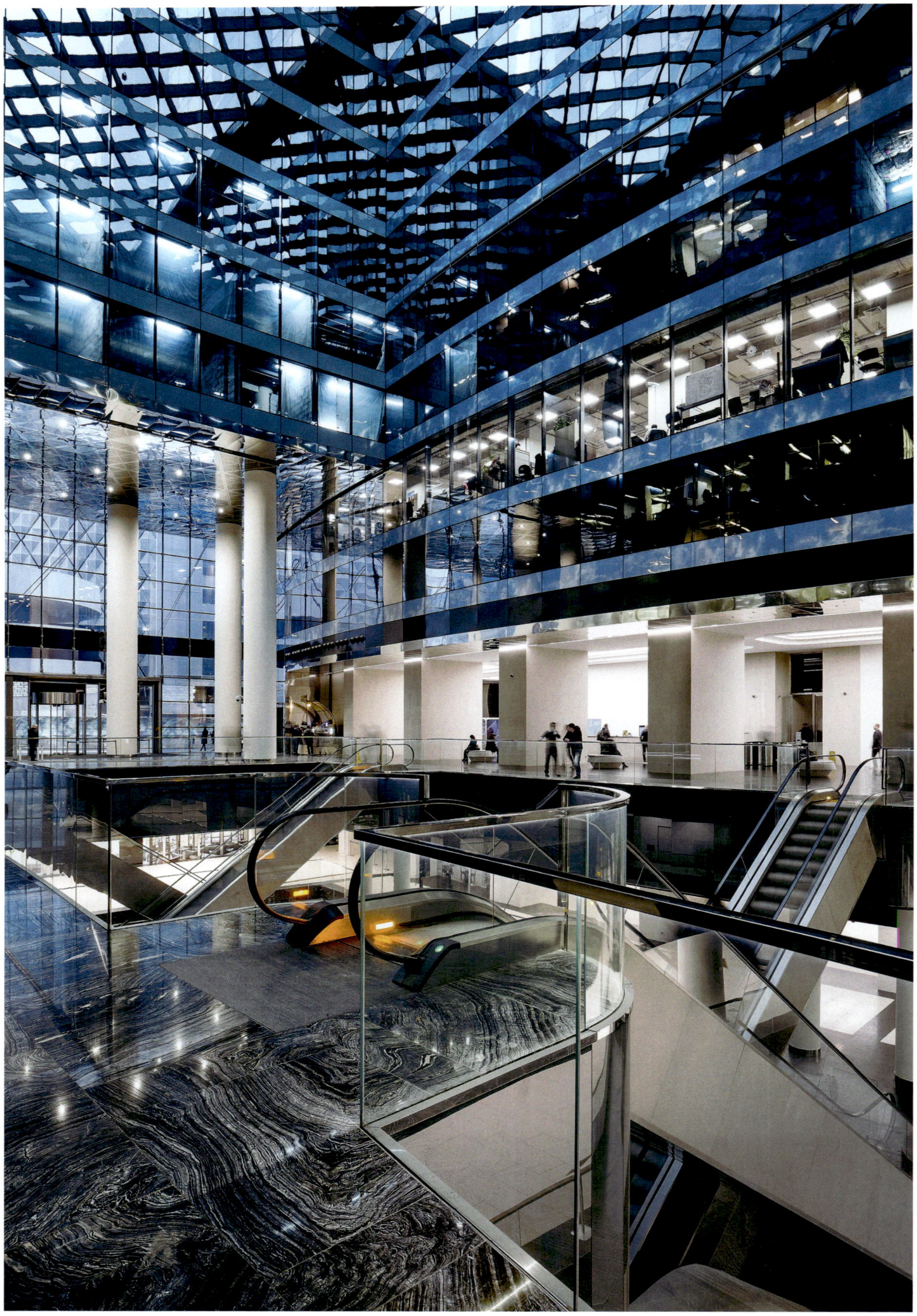

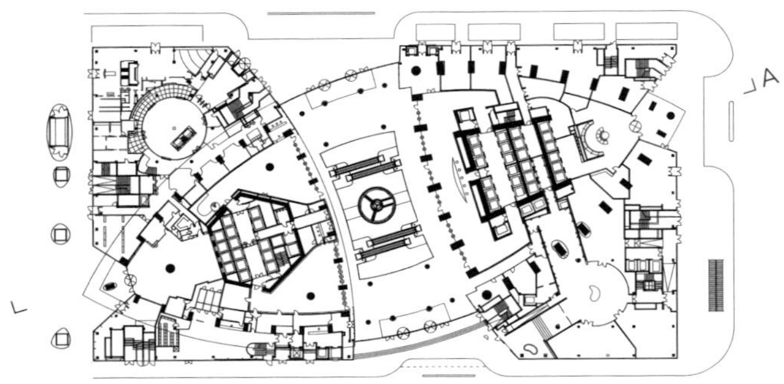

FLOOR PLAN. GROUND LEVEL

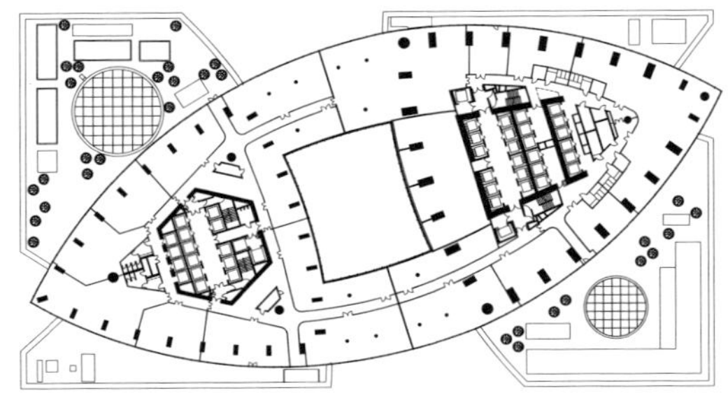

FLOOR PLAN. LEVEL 6

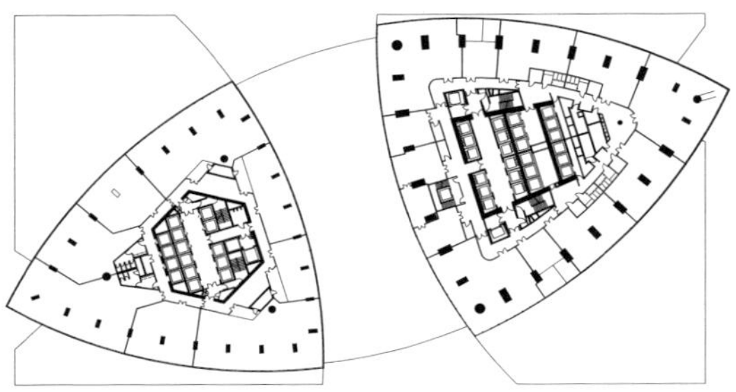

FLOOR PLAN. LEVEL 24

FLOOR PLAN. LEVEL 60

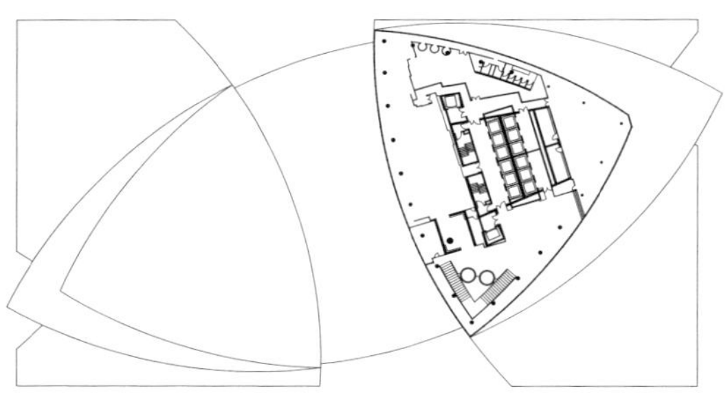

FLOOR PLAN. LEVEL 90

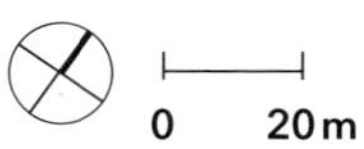

ANCHORED ON SITE: LIVING ON THE WATER IN THE MIDDLE OF THE CITY

HOUSING ON HOLZHALBINSEL

'… AN UNMISTAKABLE, DYNAMIC LANGUAGE OF FORMS THAT INTERPRETS, IN A SUSTAINABLE WAY, AN IDEA APPROPRIATE TO THE BALTIC SEA. THE THEMATIC IDEA OF 'SHAPED BY THE WIND' IMPARTS TO THE BUILDINGS AN IMAGE THAT HAS STRONG CONNECTIONS WITH THE LOCATION.

FROM THE PRESS STATEMENT BY THE JURY CHAIRED BY PROFESSOR CHRISTIANE THALGOTT

Idyllic and yet urban is how the communal housing company WIRO advertises the new island district in the Hanseatic city of Rostock. That this is not just a marketing formula is evidenced both by the special location and the architecture of this new development, completed in 2018. For this project, tucked between Rostock's historical inner city and the embankments of the River Warnow, TCHOBAN VOSS Architekten opted for a modern design that is anchored in the location and imparts to it an unmistakable identity.

Reserved in the Hanseatic manner and yet architectonically self-assertive, the residential complex on Holzhalbinsel shapes Rostock's new urban skyline. Especially distinctive are the obliquely angled roof edges and the polygonal façades of the five blocks, which are from five to nine storeys high. The architects' central idea is visible from afar: they have translated the special location on the water, where a stiff breeze often blows from the Baltic Sea, into a dynamically designed urban landscape. The almost sculptural-looking buildings and open spaces seem to have been shaped by the wind.

This was the design concept with which TCHOBAN VOSS Architekten won the architectural competition held by WIRO for the area in 2012. Holzhalbinsel is an important project for Rostock, and not just because it enriches the rental market with 181 apartments near the city center, but also because it signifies the city's expansion. Where, only 10 years ago, Rostock's old town ended beyond the medieval city walls in literally nothing more than green meadows, numerous new buildings have since sprung up. The new island neighborhood is ideally situated: what used to be a yard for storing and trading wood is now a residential district with a floor area of 13,400 square meters. To date, this is the largest project for apartment-block housing in Mecklenburg-Vorpommern.

The complex consists of four tower blocks and one 180-meter-long residential block, which borders the neighborhood in the direction of the city. The U-shape of the five- to six-storey

> ’THE WINNING DESIGN REINFORCES IN AN EXTRA-ORDINARILY CLEVER WAY THE IDENTITY OF THIS INNER-CITY DISTRICT ON THE BANKS OF THE WARNOW.
>
> FROM THE PRESS STATEMENT BY THE JURY CHAIRED BY PROFESSOR CHRISTIANE THALGOTT

block is oriented northwards, towards the Warnow, and frames a generous inner courtyard, underneath which lies an underground garage with 187 parking spaces. On the bank of the Warnow the complex is completed by three townhouses. The complex's skyline is shaped by a fifth block, a free-standing nine-storey building that rises above the five- to six-storey edge of the district. Unlike the other buildings, the high-rise has a reinforced-concrete, load-bearing framework.

The way that the buildings are arranged and grouped makes optimal use of insulation, opens up long views over the Warnow, and gives the inhabitants sufficient privacy. The diverse building types provide a range of rental options including units of 65 to 140 square meters and two-level apartments. Additionally, the development incorporates four commercial units. The ground floors are raised above street level to provide protection against flooding. The upper storeys form a band of meandering clinker façades, making a regional reference to the brick architecture of Rostock's historical inner city while continuing it in a contemporary manner.

A special challenge was the subsoil on Holzhalbinsel, which for the most part consists of artificially raised land. Throughout the development area, which was launched in 2005, road subsidence is frequent. For this reason, special measures were needed in order to make the residential area stable for the long term. 1200 foundation piles were sunk in the ground. Another special feature of this project is also in the ground: 80 geothermal loops at a depth of 110 meters serve the entire residential district, helping to make this uniquely large project a showcase for Mecklenburg-Vorpommern. ■

WWW.WARNOW-WERKSTATT.DE

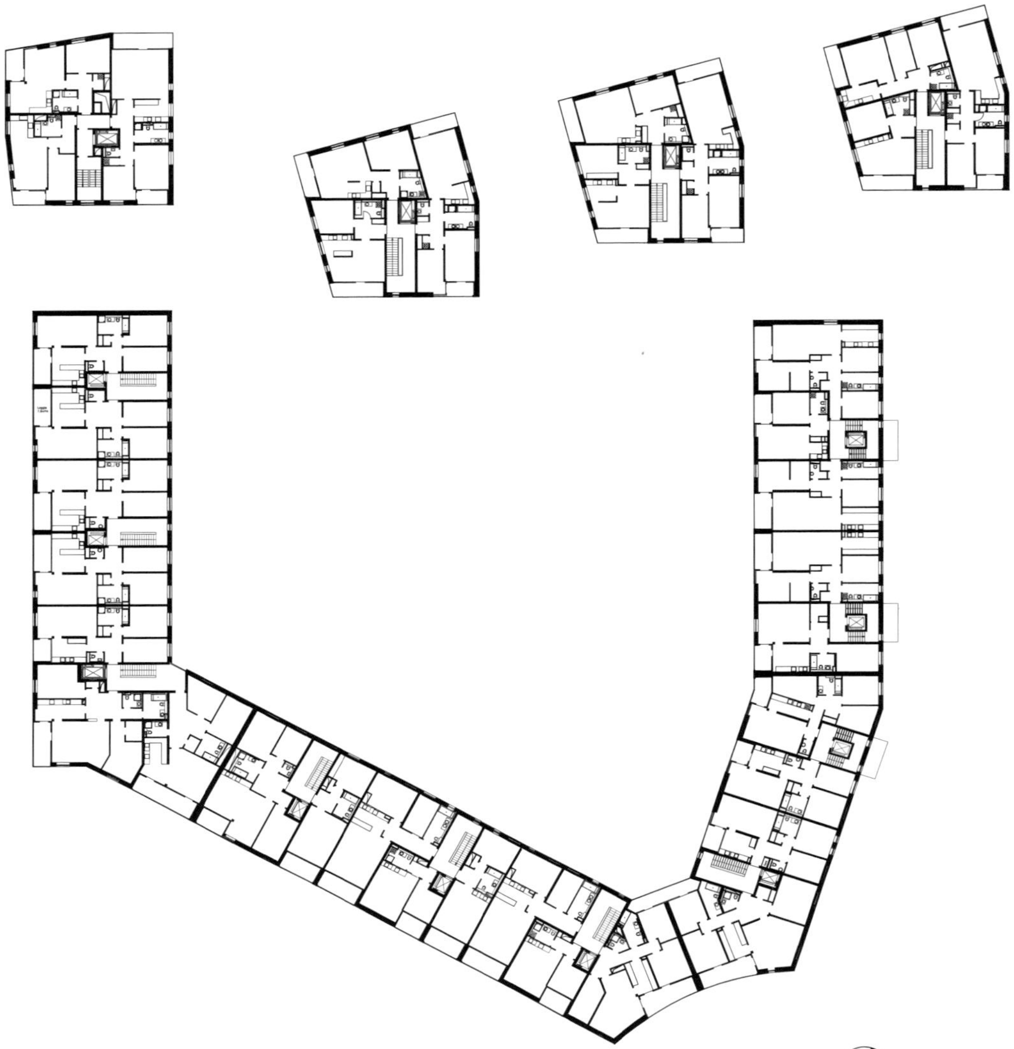

FLOOR PLAN. LEVEL 2

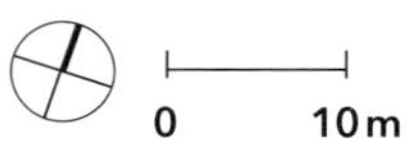

AN OFFICE BUILDING SETS AN ACCENT FOR AN URBAN BLOCK

BOXHAGENER STRASSE

' THE FAÇADE IS AN IRREGULAR GRID CONSISTING OF A DEEP AND POWERFUL RELIEF.

PROF. DR. FALK JAEGER, TAGESSPIEGEL

This distinctive office building on Boxhagener Straße draws attention to the new street block in Berlin's Friedrichshain district. The building is part of the ongoing urban development in what used to be an industrial area, a project that has led to the creation of a lively neighborhood of predominantly residential space on an approximately 26,000-square-meter site. The architects involved in the development were Bonanni Architekten, Hilmer Sattler Architekten, Lunetto Architekten, Patzschke und Partner Architekten, and TCHOBAN VOSS Architekten.

Until the late 1930s the site was occupied by Deutsche Kabelwerke AG, one of the leading manufacturers of cables for submarine communications and Berlin's S-Bahn. This company's successful development came to an end with the expropriation of its founder, Siegfried Hirschmann, under the Nazis. Production ceased and the family was forced to flee. 90 years later, Thomas Hirschmann, Siegfried's grandson, accepted an invitation to the topping-out ceremony of the new street block on April 24, 2018. He attended together with his family and is certain that his grandfather would have approved of the change and new use. The spacious garden inside the blocks bears his grandfather's name.

The office building with the distinctive corner has six full storeys and an additional set-back storey. On each floor there are four office units that can be joined together if necessary. Should tenants wish, the spatial design can be changed from open space to single-room units. New tenants appreciate this spatial freedom. The IT company SysEleven describes the attractions of its new office as, "More space, more concentration, more kitchen." In this "smart, modern building with lots of glass and a concrete façade" the employees of this constantly-growing firm have "more conference space and a relaxed living-room atmosphere for concentrated working." The international TV network Viacom International Media Networks that includes MTV, among others, is also happy with its new headquarters. The space best meets its requirements and is tailored to meet employees' needs, as Mark Sprecht, General Manager of GSA, notes in a press communication on the company's website.

The design is based on an expressive combination of glass and architectural concrete. The special façade dynamic has been achieved by the way the prefabricated concrete parts have been ordered and by differences of scale between them - an effect that the architecture critic Falk Jaeger sees as "an irregular grid consisting of a deep and powerful relief." In an article for Der Tagesspiegel Jaeger additionally emphasizes the inner spaces of the monolithic reinforced-concrete building, which impress with their "ceiling-to-floor windows," "pillar-less glazed corner rooms," and "ceilings free of any cluttering installations." The corner spaces offer a pleasant spot in which to relax, as well as impressive views; as all-glass corners, made from safety glass, they make a bold impression when viewed from the outside. According to Katharina Stranz, whose responsibilities included the façade design, and Stephan Lohre, who was project partner for this project, the development of these window elements was one of the most complex and exacting steps in the design process. Both are visibly happy with the result.

Another challenge was presented by the design of the entrance. With its warm shade of American walnut, the two-storey entrance that incorporates the door-and-bell system contrasts pleasingly with the cool light grey of the architectural concrete. The dialogue of materials continues in the two-storey lobby providing access to the building. The combination of wooden paneling and concrete surfaces looks both dignified and modern. When you glance upwards, your gaze meets not ceiling, but transparency: the first-storey glazing allows you to see inside and the mirror foil on the ceiling gives the lobby a feeling of spaciousness. ■

BOX 80

, FROM THE LARGE ROOF TERRACE WITH ITS VIEW OVER BERLIN TO DIRECT ACCESS TO LOCAL PUBLIC TRANSPORT, OUR NEW HOME OFFERS OUR EMPLOYEES **OPTIMAL CONDITIONS FOR WORKING FLEXIBLY AND CREATIVELY.**

DR. MARK SPECHT,
GENERAL MANAGER (GSA),
VIACOM INTERNATIONAL
MEDIA NETWORKS

BOX 80
PENNY.
PENNY.
PENNY.
PENNY.
PENNY.
B
O
X

BOX 80

BOXHAGENER STRASSE 80
BOX
80
BOXHAGENER STRASSE 80

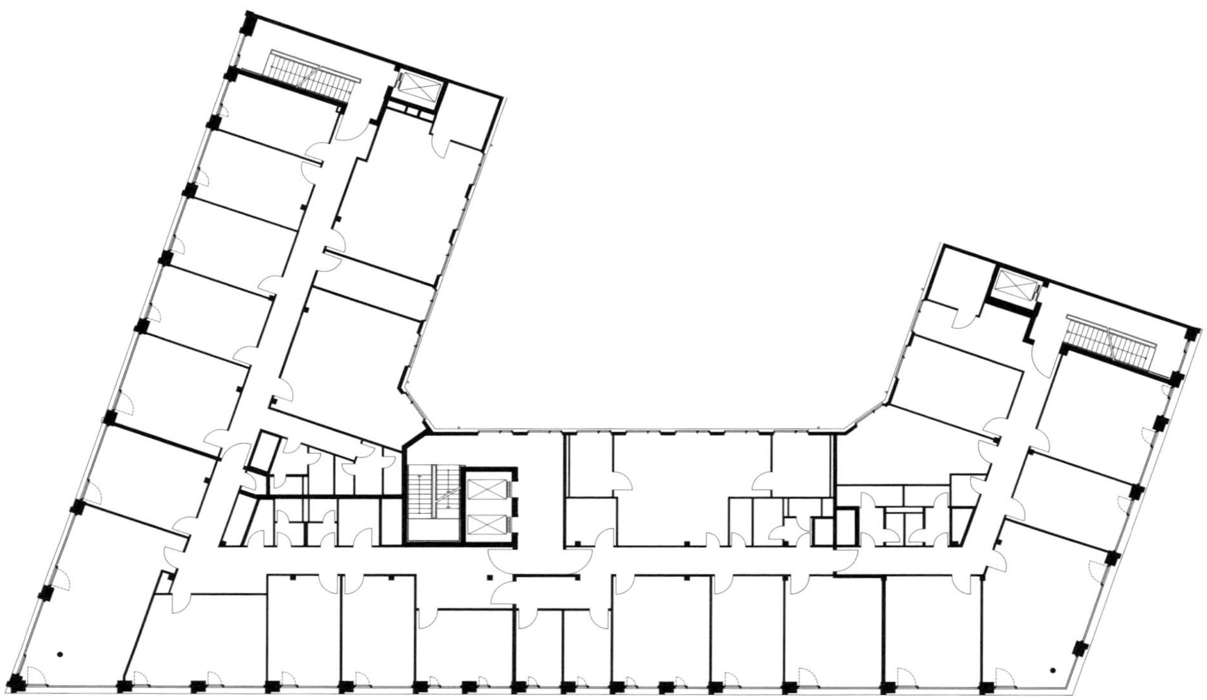

FLOOR PLAN. TYPICAL FLOOR

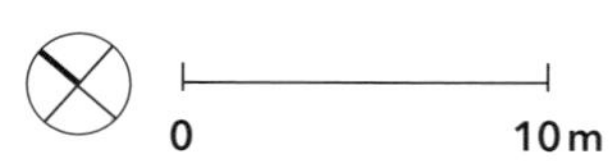

HEADED FOR NEW SHORES: A UNIVERSITY CAMPUS AS A SYMBOL AND ENGINE OF CHANGE FOR AN ENTIRE REGION

RHINE-WAAL UNIVERSITY OF APPLIED SCIENCES

ALLGEMEINE

'IN THIS LOCATION SOMETHING NEW HAS BEEN CREATED WHOSE INNOVATIVE POWER IS SHAPING THE FUTURE OF OUR REGION, BUT WITHOUT FORGETTING THE PAST. THIS IS A SYMBOL FOR THE STRUCTURAL CHANGES THAT ARE HAPPENING IN OUR REGION. AS WE HAND OVER THE KEYS, WE ARE HANDING OVER NOT JUST A MAGNIFICENT UNIVERSITY CAMPUS, BUT ALSO A NEW CITY DISTRICT OF NO SMALL SIZE FOR OUR CITIZENS.

WOLFGANG SPREEN,
MAYOR OF KLEVE

Situated in the borderland between Germany and the Netherlands, Rhine-Waal University is one of the youngest universities in Germany. It was established in 2009, with its new main campus in Kleve opening in 2012. Since then, more than 7200 students from 120 countries have made this their "study haven." The change from industrial region to knowledge center is in this case taking place not on a green-field site, but within walking distance of the city center, so as to entrench the new university in the structure of the town right from the start. The campus complex occupies an approximately 48,000-square-meter site on both sides of Germany's oldest canal, the Spoy Canal. A bridge for pedestrians and cyclists links the two campus embankments.

A reminder of this area's past function as a harbor is the former harbormaster's office and a listed storage building which is now a "knowledge store" containing 3000 meters of bookshelves, a Student Service Center on the ground floor, and a language center on one of the two upper floors. TCHOBAN VOSS Architekten argued for preserving the historical brick architecture and incorporating it in the design of the site. The 19 white new buildings on the two sides of the canal provide an attractive contrast.

The uniform design of the imposing cubes with white-lacquered metal panels and wrap-around strips of black-framed windows binds the individual buildings into a coherent ensemble. The distinctive jumps in the heights of the strips are not merely decorative: they also address the different light requirements of the buildings' specific users.

To contrast with their black-and-white exteriors, the buildings' interiors follow a design concept based on bright colors. In the individual buildings the main colors used are green, yellow, and raspberry: staircases that incorporate this color scheme create atmospheric accents and make it easier to navigate the buildings.

The auditorium building in the east of the site is the "campus forum" and the complex's spatial center. A wide, inviting staircase leads to the entrance of the 20-meter-high square building. Gold-colored walls in the foyer area and bright green in the inside of the main auditorium underscore its central function in campus life. The auditorium seats 500.

Another important meeting place is the canteen at a turning basin on the Spoy Canal. The canteen's usable roof terrace offers a panoramic view of the campus. Viewed from the terrace, the university complex looks like a small city stretched along the canal. The architects deliberately devised the development structure to be a spatially permeable system; it was this concept of a "city within a city," that led to their winning the European-wide competition for the campus design.

In this "study-haven city" open space plays an important role. In addition to the tree-lined embankment path and the campus square in front of the storage building, the architects' concept for the site includes a so-called "theme garden" between the department buildings. This was designed by landscape designer Dirk Junker. The state-of-the-art energy- and resource-saving harbor campus, to which TCHOBAN VOSS Architekten added passive-house-standard student accommodation in 2013, has, in a symbiosis of architecture and landscape design, developed into an open, green, and communicative place for students, teachers, staff, and the population of Kleve. ■

Like a small town stretching along the canal: the architects devised the buildings' layout to be a permeable, spacious system.

0
50 m

AUDIM

CORPORATE ARCHITECTURE: FROM FUNCTIONAL STRUCTURE TO LANDMARK

SVEN WINGQUIST TEST CENTER

’THE ARCHITECTS’ CONCEPT HAS BEEN A COMPLETE SUCCESS AND CREATES ADDED VALUE FOR OUR COMPANY, VALUE THAT GOES FAR BEYOND THE BUILDING’S FUNCTIONALITY.

DR. MARTIN GÖBEL, MANAGER, GLOBAL TESTING, SKF

Components of wind turbines have to withstand powerful forces and must therefore be stress-tested in preparation. The most efficient testing center in the world for large bearings - such as, for instance, rotor units for wind turbines as well as for the shipping, mining, and paper industries - has existed since the summer of 2017 in Schweinfurt. In its design for the Sven Wingquist Test Center for SKF, TCHOBAN VOSS Architekten has not merely constructed a building envelope for high-performance testing equipment. Instead of a mere functional structure, the 14-hectare site is home to a building that transforms functionality into identity-creating architecture while at the same time translating SKF's technological know-how into form and materials. The futuristic-looking design with its aerodynamic shape refers to the testing that occurs inside the structure and to the firm's corporate identity. The company logo on the façade is not only a label, but a design element that is continued in the building's rounded corners. The result is a corporate architecture suitable for a firm that is rich in tradition and ranks among the world's leading pioneers in technology.

The new testing center is named after the firm's Swedish founder, Sven Wingquist, who invented the first self-leveling bearing in 1907. Winquist's Svenska Kullagerfabriken, subsequently abbreviated to "SKF," began life with 15 employees in Göteborg. Today it has more than 80 factories all over the world and more than 45 000 employees. In Germany the company's headquarters, with approximately 4100 employees, is in Schweinfurt. Here the new testing center is expected to contribute to producing large roller bearings more efficiently, with greater economy of resources, and with greater durability. Two volumes of similar shape, each of 80 x 20 meters, stand parallel to one another, formulating the architectonic motif of the new development. The dynamic, forward-leaning, angled external design is a visualization of the forces at work inside. The testing stands in the test center can develop forces of more than one Meganewton.

The smaller, two-storey, hall contains spaces for function monitoring, storage facilities, and workshops. The heart of the test center - the testing stands - is in the taller, one-storey, hall. A 110-tonne gantry crane can be used to move extremely sensitive machine parts. The halls stand on tubular foundations. The foundation plates of both volumes, which are solid-construction with reinforced-concrete columns, were realized in reinforced concrete and fiber concrete. The façades are clad in reflective white-aluminium panels. In combination with the aerodynamic shape, the silver-sheened material gives the halls an appearance that brings to mind associations ranging from "space launch site" (BauNetz) to "high-tech monument of German engineering art" (Sebastian Remelé, mayor of Schweinfurt).

The elongated north façade of the large hall with its SKF logo is double-glazed with profiled glass. During the hours of darkness the illuminated façades create an additional connection with the high-rise administrative building several hundred meters away, which was renovated by TCHOBAN VOSS Architekten in 2014. Funded by the Bavarian Ministry for Economic Affairs and Energy and the German Ministry for the Environment, the new testing center may be regarded as a prestige project for German environmental policy. The new building has a Gold LEED certificate. In the company's view, this is "a template for SKF's communal responsibility." The testing center is on its way to becoming a new architectural landmark for the entire region. ■

SKF

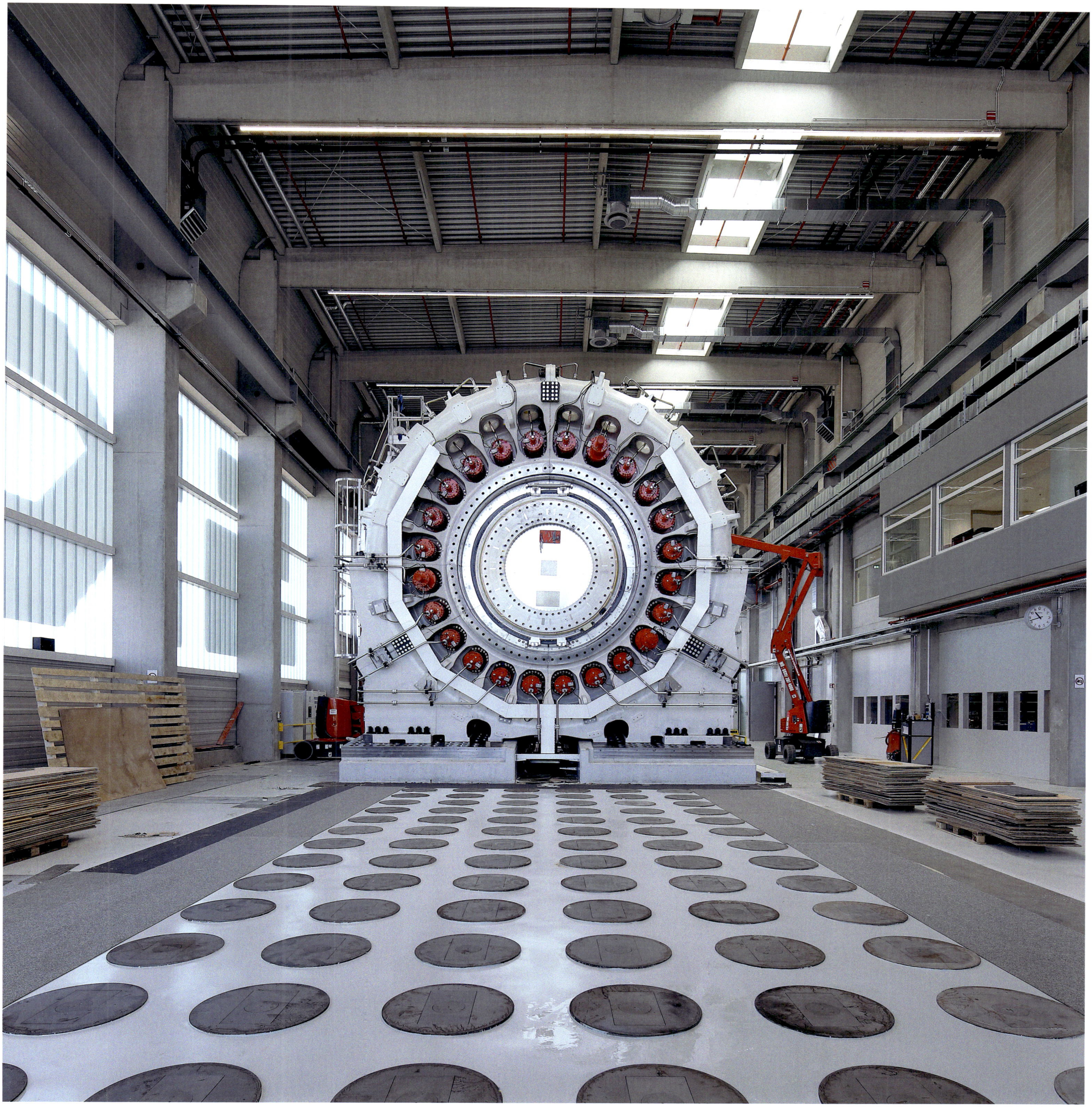

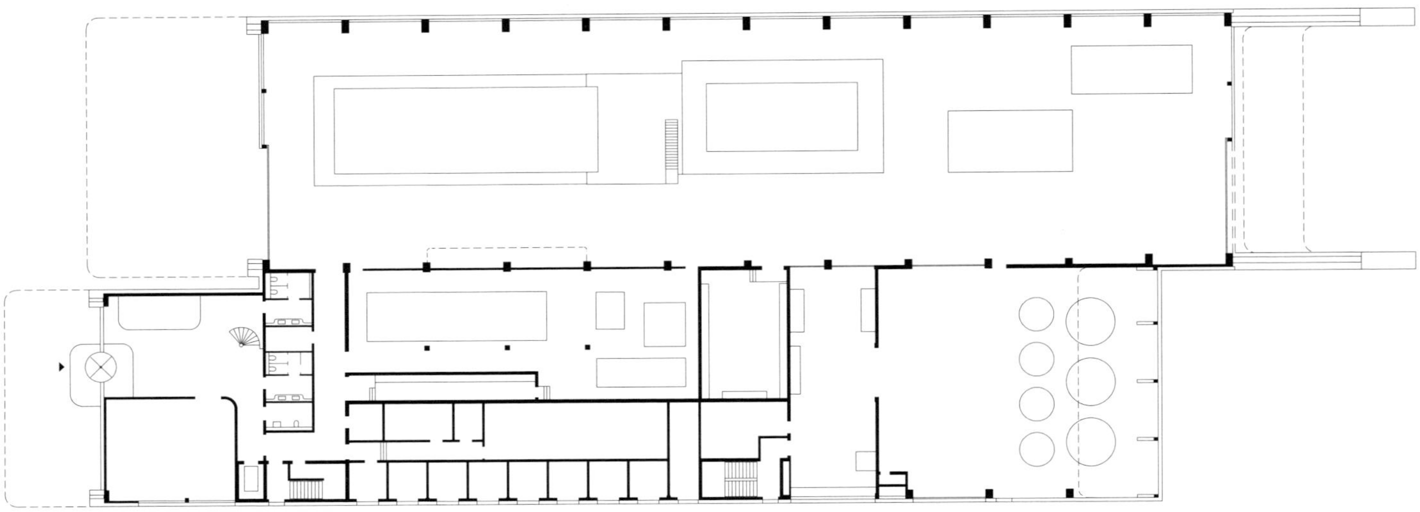

Two parallel volumes in a staggered formation establish the architectonic motif for the new development. The two-storey hall accommodates function monitoring, storage spaces, and workshops. The one-storey hall contains the test center's heart, the testing stands.

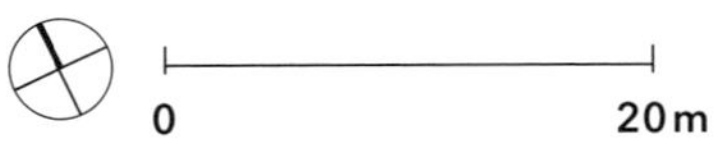

SKF

REPORT

HARBOR FLAIR AND BIG-CITY BACKDROP

THREE BUILDINGS IN BERLIN'S FORMER OSTHAFEN

BY CHRISTINA GRÄWE

Hausbootverleih Wasserkutsche.com
wasserkutsche.com
Hausbootverleih Wasserkutsche.com

A stroll along the Friedrichshainer Ufer (Friedrichshain Embankment) in Osthafen (East Harbor) on an October day redolent of late summer offers a generous helping of big-city romanticism.

Over the last decade TCHOBAN VOSS Architekten has played a significant part in shaping the new skyline on the bank of the Spree. The firm's contribution to the section south-east of Oberbaum Bridge comprises three striking buildings – the nhow music hotel, Coca-Cola's bright-red headquarters building, and an elegant apartment block, The White.

These edifices have risen up in the middle of what used to be the no man's land of the border zone, where following the fall of the Berlin wall extra sensitivity was required in handling the built heritage of the old industrial harbor. What is it like to live and work today at Osthafen in Berlin?

'Where else do you get a recording studio with a view like this?!" Eyes shining, the sound engineer gestures in the direction of the Oberbaum Bridge before launching into an explanation of the acoustically decoupled "space in space" principle. We are in the most spectacular spot in the nhow hotel, high up on a cantilever, savoring the view as if soaring above the Spree. The sound engineer has been a member of the team since nhow's opening in April 2011. His unconventional workplace is part of the hotel concept. In addition to providing rooms for guests, the nhow has a consistent focus on music, whether as an events venue or, given that it is equipped to meet the highest requirements, as a production center. In this respect the hotel operators were jumping on a bandwagon. In the immediate vicinity Universal Music Deutschland had already taken up residence in an old egg warehouse, and smaller music labels and clubs, such as the music station MTV, had settled in the area. What could be more appropriate than to combine accommodation with music in the new hotel? After all, Udo Lindenberg has been enjoying the comfort of the Atlantik in Hamburg for almost a quarter of a century and the Czech pianist Josef Bulva has been living in the Vier Jahreszeiten in Munich for 45 years.

TCHOBAN VOSS Architekten created the envelope for nhow's unusual program, an impressive volume that continues the no-less imposing row of buildings consisting of Universal's current headquarters and old storage buildings. This is the first of three buildings TCHOBAN VOSS Architekten has built in the old harbor area.

This is a district shaped by a history marked by change. Osthafen extends between Oberbaum and Elsen bridges. Between 1913 and 1939 the harbor period in its history left behind buildings typical of this time, some of which are listed as architectural monuments. In World War II the army used the facilities as a cargo-handling center.

THE THREE-STOREY CANTILEVER WITH A HOVERING SOUND STUDIO IS NHOW'S MOST SALIENT FEATURE. IT JUTS OUT 21 METERS ACROSS THE WIDER OF THE TWO RECESSES.

PRELUDE WITH MIRROR: THE NHOW MUSIC HOTEL

> ’**THE HOTEL GAINS A GREAT DEAL OF TENSION** DUE TO THE CONTRAST BETWEEN ITS HARD ENVE-LOPE AND SOFT INTERIOR.
>
> AXEL BINDER, TCHOBAN VOSS ARCHITEKTEN

When Germany and Berlin were divided, the 1.5-kilometer-long embankment strips were used for handling building materials, but also for a higher purpose – as a means of securing the border area. Watchtowers were added to the harbor buildings; other development stagnated. In the first years after the wall came down activities in this very attractive area (just think: on the water, good transport links, inner-city location) were very slow to get going. The area use plan of 2002 and subsequent development plans appealed to investors, but others feared the sale of public space. 'The Spree for all', a citizens' petition, achieved considerable popularity, calling for, among other things, the banks of the Spree to be accessible to the public. The Senate's urban-development plans for the creation of Mediaspree between Jannowitz and Elsen bridges were, however, irrevocable. Development of the area went ahead. Since then, the change from industrial harbor to haven for creativity has largely been completed. One sign of this that is visible from afar is the nhow music hotel.

The nhow gives flaneurs access to the water. The seven-storey building is predominantly clad in brick – a reminder of the façades of its immediate neighbors, the egg-storage buildings. The windows are playfully distributed over the façade; the flat masonry surfaces take their dimensions from the windows and, alternating with protruding layers of brick, result in a lively, textured exterior whose variability relieves the complex of some of its massiveness. The hotel building has three wings projecting, comb-like, towards the water. Yet with its wrap-around, fully-glazed ground floor and main entrance it does not turn its back on Stralauer Allee either. The sound of the traffic on the six-lane street fails to reach the terraces (totaling a massive 1000 square meters on three levels) overlooking the water. The three-storey cantilever with the hovering sound studio is the nhow's most salient feature, jutting out 21 meters over the wider of the two recesses. Entirely glazed on the side facing the water, it is clad in an aluminium skin pierced with windows on the other three sides. The highly-polished underside serves as a gigantic mirror. Passers-by stop, put their heads back, and start spinning around. This piece of scenery has already served as a backdrop for countless social media posts.

The impressive view from this part of the building is something that can be enjoyed by the sound engineer and his clientele and by whomever is relaxing in the bath in the 260-square-meter suite, located directly above. This two-level apartment with its own 100 square-meter terrace is, like the seven conference rooms on the ground and first floors, linked by network with the sound studio. If you don't have an instrument with you, you can either book one of the six more modest suites that are equipped with an e-piano or borrow a guitar from reception (guitars may be used in all 304 rooms).

fabrics

When it came to furnishing most of the rooms and the public spaces, including the foyer, bar, and restaurant, the operators opted for the greatest possible contrast with the angular geometry of TCHOBAN VOSS's architecture – and were given it by New York designer Karim Rashid. Here shapes flow, colors work an almost psychedelic effect, and extensive use is made of high-quality plastic and tailor-made pieces, such as the sculptural reception desk of highly polished fiber glass. A pattern based on digital representations of soundwaves stretches along the corridor walls and floors throughout the building. The raw, exposed-concrete gallery makes for a pleasant excursion. After seven years the concept still works; it is as if the décor came from a different galaxy.
Axel Binder, project partner at TCHOBAN VOSS Architekten, comments: "We found this collaboration interesting and fruitful. The hotel gains great tension through the contrast between hard envelope and soft interior." The concept derives from the extraordinary location. "Its design makes the nhow a special building, even within the NH hotel group," observes Alexander Bienefeld, the hotel's deputy director. The nhow already has true fans who have long since become regular guests.

, ITS DESIGN MAKES THE NHOW **A SPECIAL BUILDING**, EVEN WITHIN THE NH HOTEL GROUP.

ALEXANDER BIENEFELD, NHOW

COLOR PLAY IN RED: COCA-COLA DEUTSCHLAND

Further along the embankment, things continue to be colorful. The middle building in the row by TCHOBAN VOSS asserts itself against the massive nhow by means of a façade irridescent in five shades of red. At first glance, this may seem like a somewhat obvious piece of corporate design for Coca-Cola's German head office, which moved here in 2013.

However, the play of colors in fact derives from the design code set out in the concept with which TCHOBAN VOSS Architekten won the competition for the master plan in 2003. This code is oriented on variations of the terracotta color of the existing buildings that were to be incorporated into the project. Slender, rectangular ceramic panels were joined to one another horizontally, in accordance with the principle of "planned randomness," as Philip Bauer, the partner for this project, describes it. The panels are broken up by anthracite-colored areas between the windows. The façades overlooking the water are fully glazed; in front of them is a filigree structure of S-shaped steel arches, between which stretch horizontal lamellae - also in the five shades of red. This is more than decorative play: separated by slender slats, this layer serves as protection from the sun and at the same time incorporates the balcony railings. The Coca-Cola building was in the first decade of the 21st century one of the first - not just at Osthafen, but in the whole of Berlin - to make outside space part of its office space concept.

The building's use as a headquarters is reflected in the interior through a combined reception and distribution area on the ground floor, providing access to the conference rooms and canteens. The flexible open-space concept for the offices on the six upper storeys was slightly altered during the extremely short planning phase by the inclusion of acoustic walls. Transparency, however, is provided by glazed partitions. The workspaces are situated in a ring around a core containing places for coffee, meeting rooms, and niches equipped with football tables. In the foyer you can choose from over seventy drinks, including a special coffee served only in this building. Upon exiting, you are bid farewell by a Berlin Buddy Bear, in red and white of course.

,THE SHIMMERING PIXEL SURFACES WERE ASSEMBLED FROM SLENDER CERAMIC PANELS, IN ACCORDANCE **WITH THE PRINCIPLE OF 'PLANNED RANDOMNESS.'**

PHILIPP BAUER, TCHOBAN VOSS ARCHITEKTEN

HOUSE IN WHITE CURVES: THE WHITE

White – no, brilliant white – like a small ocean liner, the late-comer in the Osthafen family has been moored on the bank of the Spree since 2016. The White is a clear reference to the theme of ships and is the first residential building among the new buildings at Osthafen, which was for a long time designated as an exclusively commercial area. The leitmotif of this six-storey house, with a set-back penthouse, is the curve. Curves form the terraces on the waterfront and also define the smaller balconies (offset for the sake of the view) on the sides.

Manufacturing the prefabricated parts for the building required some sophisticated handling of concrete. On the street-facing side the curves form wing-like window apertures. Inside, the ship theme continues: fringing the full-height atrium are galleries that resemble a ship's deck with railings; they provide access to the apartments, which are between 48 and 125 square meters in size. From above, an abundance of light falls through a multi-layered membrane with built-in sun protection onto flowerbeds filled with glass pebbles and green grass – a tranquil and elegant space. Hovering at the level of the second storey is a sculpture by the artist Jovana Rusov; its design is inspired by the wingnut, but is also reminiscent of a ship's propeller.

After clearing her letterbox, a young resident talks about meeting her neighbors in the atrium and sponsoring the elliptical plant troughs that her parents have adopted. "The house," she observes with satisfaction, "has been designed really well. I like living here."

Construction on Osthafen continues at a lively pace. Ten years after "The Spree for everyone," it is clear that the citizens' initiative set in motion thinking processes that, albeit on a smaller scale than originally demanded, are becoming noticeable in the form of built structure. The embankment area is publicly accessible and popular. The new buildings do not altogether block what used to be the first row of development, but often allow through views. The tour ends where it began – on Oberbaum Bridge. A final glance over the entire area confirms that TCHOBAN VOSS Architekten has managed to walk a tightrope, contributing to the reinvention of Osthafen three unique pieces of architecture for a diversity of uses. ■

FOCUS STORIES

How do you combine under one roof protection of monuments with new use concepts? How can a piece of Russia be at home in Germany's Uckermark district? How can a swimming pool be sustainable? How can good-quality housing be created in even the smallest space? Our focus stories on nine projects from the current portfolios of TCHOBAN VOSS Architekten's offices in Berlin, Hamburg, and Dresden explore particular architectural issues and details.

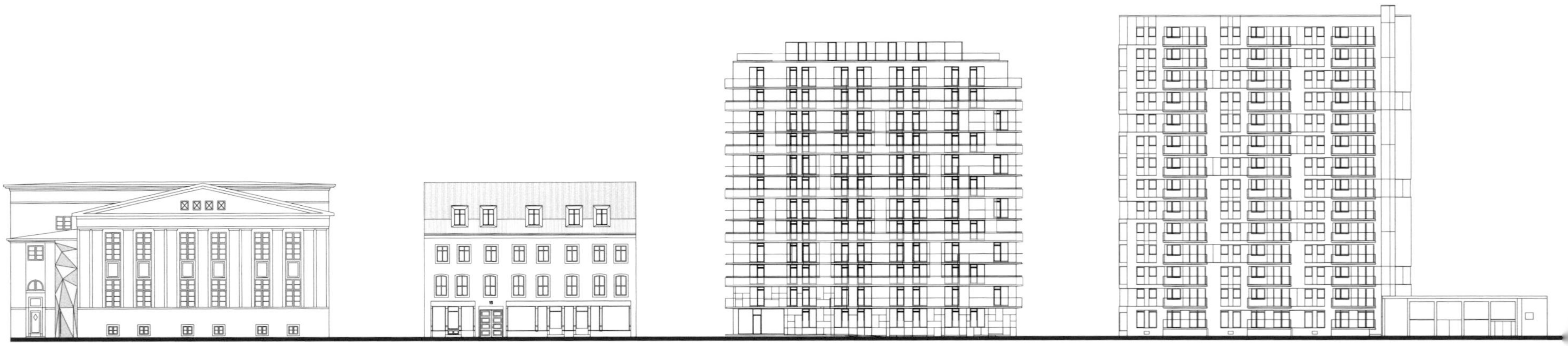

NEUE SCHÖNHAUSER 15, BERLIN

VOCATIONAL COLLEGE WITH
THREE-PITCH SPORTS HALL, GELDERN

ST. GEORG RUSSIAN
MONASTERY CHURCH, GÖTSCHENDORF

CHABAD LUBAWITSCH
SYNAGOGUE, BERLIN

LIPPE BAD LÜNEN

LIVING LEVELS, BERLIN

SCHENEFELDER HOLT, HAMBURG

NEUER HÜHNERPOSTEN
MICRO APARTMENTS, HAMBURG

STUDENT ACCOMMODATION
DRESDEN

NEUE SCHÖNHAUSER 15

DEEP-SEATED MINIMALISM

The fresh, clean appearance, the modern roofs, and newly-designed display windows: these are the things that catch the attention of the passer-by. At first you might not notice the extensive renovations carried out in the complex of buildings on Neue Schönhauser Straße in Berlin. But closer inspection of the complex, which was begun in the middle of the 18th century and successively extended into the side wings, reveals the scale of the redesign.

A particular challenge faced by the architects was that both this building and the entire Spandauer Vorstadt, of which it is a part, are protected by conservation regulations. Neither on the street side nor in the courtyard could any changes be made. The project called for a sort of cautious minimalism.

But how could these constraints be reconciled with the wishes of the current occupants? How could a sensibly-structured commercial space be created under such conditions? The solution was in the basement: in agreement with municipal authorities, the cellar spaces were extended in terms of both area and height by dropping the floor. The entire courtyard area now has a basement underneath it, giving the commercial tenant the space it needs, while the value and appearance of the building have hardly been affected.

Almost as invisible and unobtrusive as the extensive renovations is the addition of a small extension in the courtyard. This new structure has a light-grey façade of white-washed brick – a dignified addition to the complex that speaks a modern architectural language all its own. ■

The extension's clinker-brick façade fits unobtrusively into the ensemble of listed buildings.

YELLOWKORNER
15
& other Stories
-30%
IKKS FRIENDS

Berufskolleg Geldern
des Kreises Kleve

VOCATIONAL COLLEGE WITH THREE-PITCH SPORTS HALL

A POLIS FOR EDUCATION

The cube of channel glass contrasts with the solid base, especially at night.

Geldern, a town with a population of nearly 34 000, has a new vocational college – an additional urban component consisting of public buildings that ensure a mixture of architectural structures in the town's new district in the vicinity of Nierspark. The complex accommodates diverse uses – from study and workshop spaces to a library, a teaching center, and a sports hall. The new group of buildings is united by the architectural language of early-Modernist industrial buildings. The keynote of the design is the façade's charcoal-fired brick cladding in conjunction with the use of translucent glass elements.

To accommodate changing usage, the layouts are all flexible. The thoughtful integration of color into the design provides good navigation and replaces the usual school atmosphere with that of a place of creativity and communication. A small park – replete with a pond, zones with lush vegetation, seating, and lounge areas – frames the central approach to the vocational college, creating spaces for relaxation outside the school.

The main feature of the three-pitch sports hall with seating for 216 is its eye-catching translucent cube. Whereas the socle storey is solid and, in harmony with the other buildings in the complex, lined with dark brick, the cladding of the reinforced-concrete superstructure is predominantly of Profilit channel glass. At night the cube lights up, making the sports hall – and the entire complex of buildings – visible from afar. ■

ST. GEORG RUSSIAN MONASTERY CHURCH

SACRAL SYMBIOSIS

To build a Russian Orthodox church in Protestant Brandenburg is a demanding brief that requires sensitivity. Mention of a Russian church might make you think of St. Basil's on Red Square: how could this diversity of shapes and colors be compatible with Protestant modesty? Not all Russian Orthodox churches are as ostentatious as St. Basil's, however. There are numerous examples of more modest design: think of churches in northern and central Russia, for instance.

The church was the idea of Norbert Kuchinke. After working for many years as a news correspondent in Moscow in the 1970s Kuchinke became known for his part in a classic Russian film. Years later he struck on the idea of setting down a piece of Russia in Germany's Uckermark region – in the form of a monastery. He approached Sergei Tchoban with a proposal to translate his concept into architecture. Numerous rounds of consultations with the Berlin diocese of the Russian Orthodox Church and several years of construction bore fruit in the inauguration of a simple church on a plot of land surrounded by forested low hills in Götschendorf in Uckermark in 2017.

With three apses in the altar area, the four-gabled volume has, in keeping with Russian tradition, no socle storey. Although this is in many ways a typical Byzantine-Russian type of church, complete with a circular lantern and onion dome, what marks it as unique is its elegant simplicity. The church's charm lies in the thoughtful use of simple, but attractive details. Light-colored, whitewashed brickwork gives off, depending on the light, a light-silver or golden sheen; the light-grey wooden roof shingles appear metallic in the sunlight. The double jambs around the main door arch, the window surrounds, a staggered impost, and lesenes on the main façade impart depth to the façade. Slender vertical windows emphasize the building's sacral character. ■

The façade gains depth from the double walls around the main doorway arch and from the window surrounds and pilaster strips.

SYMBOL OF DIVINE AUTHORITY

Behind the light-colored classical façade, which once fronted an electricity substation and more recently a laboratory for street lighting, there is now a "dynamic and open platform for Jewish culture, living, and tradition," as Chabad Lubawitsch Berlin aptly puts it. Handed over to this Jewish Orthodox community for a period of 99 years, the building erected by Otto Hanke in 1922 in Berlin has become a modern cultural center.

The building was not protected by any historical preservation regulations; instead of being renovated, it might just as easily have been demolished. The architects decided on a gentle approach to the existing structure that combined the external envelope with the new use. To welcome visitors, a glass installation in the colors of the tallit was placed in the entrance area. The graceful simplicity of the interior provides a gentle transition from the outside world. A feeling of security and trust is celebrated: the connecting wall between the foyer and the synagogue is clad, in an echo of the Wailing Wall in Jerusalem, with monolithic blocks of sandstone. Soft, arched elements define the overall concept, from the entrance hall, with its drop-shaped seating and lighting compositions, to the synagogue itself – a walnut-panelled, tranquil space, whose warm brown and claret colors are additionally defined by the lines running along the walls and details like the women's gallery, the lectern, and an asymmetrically placed pillar. In addition to the irregularly positioned lighting strips, there is an oval skylight – a natural light source that suggests a link with the divine. ■

The glass installation in the entrance area is the only sign of the careful conversion of the electrical substation originally designed by Otto Hanke.

LIPPE BAD LÜNEN

PILOT PROJECT FOR SUSTAINABILITY

Construction oriented on the disabled, use of regenerative energy (biogas district heating), a thermal shell that reduces heat losses, and, thanks to improved air humidity, evaporation: the first passive-house indoor swimming pool to be built in Germany has made a big impression with its combination of sustainable construction and architectonic quality. The new building saves more than 50 percent energy every year compared to its precursor.

This "ecological lighthouse project", as Dr. Wulf Grimm, head of the Department of Environmental Technology at Deutschen Bundesstiftung Umwelt (DBU), called it at its opening, was designed to serve 230,000 visitors every year. The new building replaces two indoor swimming pools and incorporates in its structure, after dismantling and renovation, an existing district heating system. From the point of view of urban planning, this was the initial impulse for converting what used to be commercial space in this central location.

The building welcomes visitors with a projecting canopy leading to a large entrance area; the canopy is supported by an angled pillar. The roof structure consists of laminated timber and prefabricated wooden acoustic ceiling elements. The thermal envelope consists of roof-and-floor slab insulation as well as a high-quality wood-and-aluminium mullion/transom façade with triple glazing.

The interior spaces are bright and, thanks to the generous window fronts, enjoy abundant daylight. Visitors can choose between five pools, including a toddler pool, a hot pool, a recuperation pool, and a pool with a lifting floor. With 839 square meters of water, the passive-house indoor swimming baths in Lünen cater to the needs of nearly every type of swimmer. ■

Efficiency even in the swimming pool: ultra-filtration and inline chlorination eliminate the need to store hazardous materials.

LIPPE
BAD
ruhe

LIVING LEVELS

DISTANT VIEWS, WHITE TOWER

The high mica content of the façade coating reinforces the three-dimensional play of shapes.

It all comes together here: formerly a busy harbor and warehouse area, the embankment of the Spree not far from the Ostbanhof later became a death strip and finally an abandoned wasteland. Today Berliners and tourists associate this area with the colorful East Side Gallery.

Just a few years ago, it would have been almost impossible to imagine housing in this spot. The spectacular high-rise right on the water's edge is the first residential building to be erected here; it was completed in 2015. Standing adjacent to the site of the Brommy Bridge, which was blown up during WWII but is now to be rebuilt, this sculptural volume brings to the cityscape a new feeling. This is not Baudelaire's Berlin of the 1990s, but a pulsating metropolis.

The almost continuously glazed façades of the 14-storey, 63 meter-high building are a reflection of the building's internal structure, whose concrete load-bearing framework with a reinforced concrete core and metal façade give absolute freedom in the design of the apartment layouts. Panoramic views of the Spree and the city make the residential spaces seem almost infinite. The meandering two-storey framing of the bay windows has already become a recognizable feature.

Sustainability, however, is a matter not just of flexible layouts. It is also fundamental to the building's utilities. The latter includes heating provided by a combination of cogeneration of heat and electricity and a concrete-core activation system. The planting of vegetation on the embankment is continued on the façade in the form of trees - planted in special tubs made for this purpose and installed on the terraces. ■

TEST THE REST

The contemporary surface relief overlies the existing façades, giving them a new structure.

SCHENEFELDER HOLT

NEW IMAGE

The new façade for the Schenefelder Holt residential complex in the Iserbrook district of Hamburg has won Brillux's German Façade Award twice. The 14-storey high-rise residential block from the 1960s took First Prize in 2012. In an anniversary retrospective in 2016, the project won an additional award as one of the best works from recent years.

The aging residential complex was no longer acceptable to its inhabitants or neighbors. Today, together with the two low, new satellite buildings, it looks lively and colorful. It was this enhancement of its setting that was stressed by the jury in the reasons it gave for its award: "Only when you picture the state of the façade before and after the energy-conservation project can you appreciate the enormous added value in terms of design that this modernization has given."

The sculptural, even playful façade relief is defined by colored Alucobond panels and a high-contrast color scheme consisting of sand, red, white, and black. In terms of energy conservation, the reticular thermal-insulation system allows the building to conform to the most modern sustainability requirements. The Alucobond panels can also be found in the façades of the two flanking row buildings. The latter contain, in addition to local supplies and service facilities, a total of 24 apartments, some of which are two-level with direct access from the courtyard. ■

NEUER HÜHNERPOSTEN MICRO APARTMENTS

CENTRAL MICRO APARTMENTS FOR TEMPORARY USE

Specialist discussion regarding the increasing minimization of square meters in our apartments has in recent years flowed on the pages of our daily and weekly newspapers. Proposals for future housing have included such things as "tiny houses," increased spatial efficiency, and modular dwellings. Such discussions are hardly new. In 1984 an Italian comedy classic showed a new resident in Milan proudly enthusing about his 10 square meter apartment with sliding doors and a mini folding bed. Today, as then, immigration, demand that outstrips supply, and consequent housing shortages are common in big cities.

Creating a pleasant dwelling in a space of 20 square meters is now all in a day's work for architects. In an absolutely central location in Hamburg's Hühnerposten district, TCHOBAN VOSS Architekten have designed a new building with micro apartments for temporary use. The triangular block is part of an ensemble of five buildings whose acute angles establish a design connection with Fritz Höger's iconic Chilehaus. The group of buildings is based on Meurer Architekten's winning project for the urban-planning competition of 2001.

The twelve-storey building contains 342 one-room and 11 two-room apartments with a floor area of 19 square meters each, arranged compactly along a central corridor. Fitted with a shower, a bed, a desk, a cupboard or shelves, and a mini-kitchen, the apartments spare the emerging type of city dweller - fast, smart, very busy - the trouble of having to worry over how to furnish their apartment. ■

Top: continuous balcony strips girdle the courtyard façades. Bottom: the dominant element here is the relief-type cladding with its contrast of light and dark.

gesperrt!

STUDENT ACCOMMODATION DRESDEN

LIVING IN THE NEUSTADT

All-in-one concept: all 199 apartments are fully furnished.

If you climb onto the roof terrace, enthuses project manager Christoph Schröter, you can enjoy a breathtaking sight – a view far across the city, even across the whole of Dresden, from one side to the other of the Elbe Valley and, when visibility is good, right up to the Elbe Sandstone Mountains. Students who have moved in since the building was completed in 2016 also have the benefit of, in addition to the view from the spacious and furnished terrace, an all-in-one concept in the 199 one-room apartments. All the apartments are fully furnished, equipped with an open kitchen and their own bathroom module, and offer students the opportunity to concentrate on their studies – or on Dresden's hip Neustadt ("New Town") district.

In terms of urban planning, the new building cleverly fits into the existing development on Holzhofgasse and Bautzener Straße. The alignments and dimensions of the surrounding buildings have been adopted and continued on both streets and in the internal courtyard. Taken together, this makes the five-storey edge of the street block an imposing ensemble with a touch of Parisian flair. The external design is rounded off with French windows, emphasized by recessed surrounds, and with a noble-grey color scheme on the façades, restrained rustication in the socle area, and finally with the dark-grey roof tiles of the mansards.

A load-bearing structure consisting of columns instead of bearing walls makes future changes of use in the southern wing especially easy to carry out. If desired, the units can be converted to larger apartments without the need for fundamental changes to the building shell. ■

REPORT

THIS IS HOME – FOR A LIFETIME

A VISIT TO BETHANIEN-HÖFE IN HAMBURG

BY FRANZISKA EIDNER

The generation of people aged 65+ is growing. In Germany they now make up more than 20 percent of the overall population. Everyone wants to lead a dignified and, if possible, independent life as long as possible. Whether a retirement home can serve its neighborhood as a place for people to meet and whether a care home can be a proper home depends, above all, on the people who work there. However, the building can also play a part, as is shown by a visit to the Bethanien-Höfe (Bethany Courtyards) in Eppendorf.

The middle of the day, at a quarter to 12, in the Hamburg district of Eppendorf. Pausing for a while before entering the Bethanien-Höfe, it is best to position yourself on the opposite side of the street, in front of the entrance to what used to be the Bethany Hospital. From here you get a good first impression of the new retirement home and care facility which opened in spring 2015; but that is not all. A glance at the glazed bridge that links two of the three buildings of the diaconal complex reveals something about how the new building is grounded in its neighborhood, its tradition-rich prehistory, and the Christian sense of security that the Bethanien-Höfe wishes to impart to its residents.

A handful of elderly women in hoods and habits are walking to lunch. For decades they were deaconesses serving in the spirit of Christian charity in Bethany hospitals and care facilities in Hamburg, Berlin, Chemnitz, and Plauen; now they live in the new convent at Bethanien-Höfe (where previously there stood a convent built in 1904). "I'm finally back home," says one of the nuns. This feeling of being at home is, of course, only natural given that the nuns have returned to their workplace, which they left for the duration of the construction work. It also, however, arises from the architecture of this complex of buildings. This is architecture that clearly positions itself as contemporary, while at the same time suggesting ideas of participation and community and making references to local tradition.

The Bethanien-Höfe complex consists of three interlinked blocks of four to six storeys. A walkway and four internal courtyards open up diverse meeting places. And a recurring wave theme serves as a Hanseatic/maritime design element, creating design highlights and associational emphases.

The courtyards of the Bethany Deaconesses Foundation combine residential accommodation for the elderly with support and care. In addition to a home with 68 two- and three-room apartments for assisted living, there is an inpatient care facility with 123 nursing places in nine residential groups, including a secured living area for people with dementia. The complex also includes a new convent with 21 apartments for the Bethany deaconesses and spaces for a community of the Evangelical Methodist Church. 225 people between the ages of 65 and 95 years-old live at the Bethanien-Höfe, in addition to which there are 90 employees to look after and care for them.

That a new residential development was even possible here, in this traffic-congested location on Ring 2, is only due to the conclusion of an urban-planning agreement and adherence to strict noise ordinances.

BETHANIEN-HÖFE EPPENDORF

'THE COVERED WALKWAY IS A SYMBOL OF PARTICIPATION: IT ENCLOSES THE SHELTERED MIDDLE, WHICH IN TURN OFFERS OPENNESS TOWARDS THE SKIES.

EKKEHARD VOSS

TCHOBAN VOSS Architekten's involvement in the project began at the concept-development phase for the site. The Bethanien-Höfe are operated by Agaplesion Bethanien Diakonie, a sister company of the Bethany Deaconesses Foundation. TCHOBAN VOSS Architekten had already designed a facility for these two partners in Berlin and was only too happy to be involved in the new project.

For Ekkehard Voss creation of the courtyards was a "labor of love." This is especially noticeable when you hear him speak about the central design element – the covered walkway. For his degree he wrote a thesis on the architecture of monasteries. Voss studied at Aachen under Gottfried Böhm, whose post-war Modernist religious buildings earned him the status of architectural legend. That was several decades ago; however, the enthusiasm with which this experienced-planner speaks of the symbolism and practicality of the architecture of Bethanien-Höfe for daily life could belong to that of a young graduate. "It's great," he comments, "when a spatial idea also has symbolic value and is accepted as such. The covered walkway is a symbol of participation: it encloses the sheltered middle, which in turn offers openness towards the skies." While the motif of the covered walkway is based on the building's Christian foundations, the idea of different courtyards came from local features of the site. On the plot there stood an enormous beech tree that the architects were determined to preserve. In the end, however, they had to remove the tree for logistical reasons, something that Ekkehard Voss regrets to this day. It was important for him that a new tree should be planted to replace it and that it should look as if it had always stood here.

This is the impression you get if you enter the entrance courtyard from Martinistraße. The tree is surrounded by a circular raised flowerbed with a bench running continuously round it. This is a welcome resting place for the congregation of the evangelical Methodist church after weekend services. On the left side of the entrance courtyard you come to Martini, a public restaurant where you will find not only residents, but also afternoon visitors from the neighborhood. Being open to the surrounding district was from the beginning part of the concept for this building, as were the flea markets that are held regularly here and bring hundreds of Eppendorfers bustling through the grounds of the Bethanien-Höfe.

The restaurant seats 70 and is part of Building 1, which houses the care home. Building 2, to the right of the entrance courtyard, contains apartments for deaconesses and community spaces. Building 3, which is connected to Building 2, accommodates the retirement home.

The main façade material is red-brown exposed brickwork in various shades of red – a reference to the history of this spot, but also a factor in integrating the Bethanien-

THE RIGHT BALANCE OF FREEDOM AND SECURITY FOR RESIDENTS IS ONE OF THE FUNDA- MENTAL CARE PRINCIPLES AT BETHANIEN- HÖFE.

Höfe with the surrounding development (in the immediate vicinity, across the street, stands the former Bethany Hospital, a listed building). At the same time, the reduced use of materials and the structure of the buildings refer to the present day.

To emphasize the complex's coherence of content in a formal way, the architects deliberately refrained from using chromatic differentiation in the exteriors of the individual blocks. Seen from the internal courtyard, Building 1 – also known as "Bethanien-Haus" – stands out from the other buildings in terms of façade design. Above the ground floor, the façades in the inner courtyard have been plastered in a light color, to prevent the courtyard from seeming too dark. The windows in the care home extend down to the floor; the apartments for deaconesses and the assisted-living apartments have windows fitted with low parapets. The living rooms open onto balconies, loggias, and terraces through floor-length glazing. The recessed façade areas of the loggias and terraces have light-colored plaster surfaces, in contrast with the colors of the dark masonry façade.

In addition to being drawn to the brickwork and the covered walkway, visitors find their attention repeatedly seized by the central design motif, even before they enter the courtyard. Wave elements made from steel sheets are attached to the external façade. Originally, these were designed as enclosed bay windows in order to reduce noise. The noise-reduction function, however, has been taken over by elaborate window structures. The waves have nevertheless remained in place for reasons of urban design – especially since what was originally a functional element is aesthetically attractive. The waves create a sculptural rhythm that contrasts with the buildings' rectangular geometry and makes the façade "swing." Entering the courtyard, visitors to the building find repeated instances of the wave motif – in the canopies of the building entrances, in the balcony railings, and in the covered walkway. The waves were made from mass-produced concrete elements; Beate Schonlau, project manager for this project and TCHOBAN VOSS Architekten's expert in barrier-free access, is evidently proud of them. Implementation in concrete presented a challenge in terms of production technology; in fact, it was almost decided to use steel panels instead. But thanks to Beate Schonlau's tenacity – a quality which is immediately noticeable when you go round the building – and the concrete manufacturer's willingness to experiment, a solution was nevertheless found.

That the concrete work would in places be decorated with strings of lights was, of course, not foreseen by the architects. However, even if Beate Schonlau might have preferred the concrete to adhere to Purist principles, she is happy about this detail since it shows that the building has been accepted by its users and its architecture is fit for daily use. This is especially important for Schonlau who has worked for TCHOBAN VOSS Architekten for more than 20 years. It is why she went back to her studies to become a specialist in barrier-free construction and, together with a colleague, advises on all of the firm's buildings in matters of barrier-free access. "Buildings must be accessible and usable by all," she says. "Barrier-free access is an important design task." This has also led to her being involved as an expert at DIN e.V., the German Institute for Standardization.

It goes without saying that the entire complex of buildings at Bethanien-Höfe is barrier-free. All three buildings have lifts that are accessible to wheelchairs and suitable for carrying freight. There are four charging stations for electric cars or wheelchairs. The doors for the entrances to the buildings and the underground garage and for the staircases and lifts are fitted with electrical door drives. The retirement home has a wheelchair room that is accessible from both inside and outside.

So much for foreseeable standards. What, however, surprises when you walk around the retirement home - especially, the care home - since it does not conform to usual expectations, is the homely atmosphere, the designer details. The wave motif makes a reappearance in the curtains and carpets. Furthermore, a design concept has been developed for each individual building, with TCHOBAN VOSS Architekten also taking responsibility, together with WIBU Nord-West GmbH, for the interior design. "I know every curtain here and every single skirting board," jokes Beate Schonlau. And when you walk through the buildings, it is clear that this is indeed the case. What immediately strikes you is that all the corridors in the care home are fitted with heavy red carpets. There are numerous seating areas with sofas, creating a "homely atmosphere." Nina Hoyer-Seibert, who is in charge of nursing services, was initially sceptical about whether the carpets would stand the test of everyday use. Now she is satisfied: for many residents the carpets are something familiar that they know from their former living environment, creating a warm and pleasant atmosphere and allowing them to walk through the corridors in their socks. They feel at home.

> ’IT'S GREAT WHEN A SPATIAL IDEA ALSO HAS SYMBOLIC VALUE AND IS ACCEPTED AS SUCH.
>
> EKKEHARD VOSS

> **EVERYTHING HERE IS SO CLOSE TOGETHER,** THE RESIDENTS OF THE RETIREMENT HOME AND OF THE CARE HOME ARE NOT SEPARATED, AND VISITORS FROM THE NEIGHBORHOOD ARE ALWAYS WELCOME.
>
> JEANNINE STROZYNSKI, MANAGEMENT BETHANIEN-HÖFE

"The right balance of freedom and security for our residents" is one of the fundamental care principles at Bethanien-Höfe. This is also true of the door leading to the dayroom on the residential floor for residents with dementia. Well-thought-out safety measures on this floor allow residents to come and go freely. Nina Hoyer-Seibert also proudly shows the garden on the roof terrace – a gem of landscape design that has been taken to heart by residents, visitors, and staff alike: a place with a feel-good factor. This is also true of the bath in each care unit. Here too the architects took great care of every detail. "We wanted to create not a sterile functional space, but a place with a good feeling," says Beate Schonlau.

What is true of the nursing area plays an even greater role in Building 3, where the residents live autonomously in their apartments. Here, in addition to the four walls themselves, residents have at their disposal a clubroom, a fitness area, a swimming pool, and a sauna with outside terrace. For Jeannine Strozynski, who runs Building 3 with its elderly people's home, it is especially important to underline how the architecture creates opportunities for meeting outside of the buildings, too. "Everything here is so close together," she observes, adding, "The residents of the elderly people's home and the care home are not separated, and visitors from the neighborhood are always welcome." As we stroll along the walkway to the exit, Jeannine Strozynski points to the bench that, extending all the way round the courtyard, is an invitation to linger on the restaurant terrace or to visit the large events hall in Building 2, where choir rehearsals and film evenings take place. She talks proudly of the more than 25 volunteers from the neigborhood. And of the numerous people who regularly ask for information about the possibility of coming to live at Bethanien-Höfe, she notes, "Word has got about that this is a home – for a lifetime." ■

FEATURE TOPICS

WORK ENVIRONMENTS. DEVELOPMENT. HOTELS. HOUSING.

Building housing is one of the most important tasks in architecture today; Christina Gräwe looks at four projects that represent the rich variety of briefs realized by TCHOBAN VOSS Architekten in this field. Another focus for the office is designing new work and retail spaces; Tim Berge illuminates the challenges that architects face and to which architecture must respond, following changes in how we work and shop. Jasmin Jouhar writes on hotel projects, a field in which TCHOBAN VOSS Architekten also sees high quality and durability as key. And Luise Rellensmann considers four renovation projects demonstrating how the same principles are embodied in the firm's approach to development of existing buildings.

SPACES FOR NEW THINKING

The workplace of the future puts the focus on people. This calls for new and holistic design methods that take account of the natural environment and social surroundings and create space for the mind and body.

BY TIM BERGE

Almost no other type of building seems to have undergone such pronounced change as the architecture of the workplace. There is a simple reason for this: digitalization, social change, and scientific innovation have transformed our everyday lives and our needs – and with them the kinds of jobs we do and the places in which we do them. Nowhere is the influence of technological acceleration greater than in modern offices and service areas, regardless of whether these are administrative offices, start-ups, shopping malls, or factories. And nowhere are there stronger and more comprehensive requirements concerning health, sustainability, and users' well-being. This is the story of a breathtaking evolution towards a new architecture of work.

THE WORLD OF THE OFFICE ON THE MOVE

The 21st century brought not just a new millennium, but also the beginning of two movements that have changed everything: the digital revolution and the ecological revolution. The former was made possible by new and, above all, low-cost technologies, that connect people not only with one another but also with machines. Digitalization has affected the new industries and the classic types of jobs. More and more people are doing work tasks outside the traditional workplace and working hours – on their way somewhere, at home, or in a co-working space. The boundaries between work and private lives are becoming increasingly blurred: the office is where we are.

However, considerations of "sustainability" have also, albeit more subtly than digitalization, changed the working day and work architecture and the way that many businesses think and behave. This is a matter of ecological and economic sustainability. Office and commercial buildings must be able to cope with the unpredictability of the real-estate market and with social change – especially at a time when such change is happening increasingly quickly and unpredictably. And since immovable property, as the term itself indicates, is not mobile, its contents must be. Office buildings have to be able to react quickly to the variable and constantly changing world of work. The basis for this is an adaptable architecture with flexible space management.

The classic workplace, however, still has an important part to play. Ideally, a work space embodies a company's spirit and identity and imparts to employees a strong sense of its culture. In it experiences can be created that bind together employees and employers. This is a real asset at a time when digitalization and virtual reality are increasingly loosening real ties between people. Also true is that the higher the quality of an office, the greater its attraction for employees and young talent. This is something shown by recent surveys. When a UK furniture supplier, Furniture at Work, surveyed 2000 workers throughout Europe as to which criteria their "ultimate" office should fulfill, the most frequent answers included ceiling-to-floor windows, an abundance of light, and a beautiful view. Employees want a healthy work environment and to feel at ease in their office. Only under such conditions are they motivated to devote a large part of their time and energy to a company.

JOINT MISSION

If architects are intent on fulfilling all the criteria for a modern workplace, they need a client who supports a holistic approach to design. Well thought-out office worlds can only arise when there is a "red thread" running through the entire design and planning process - from integration into the urban context to architectural design and the furnishing and presentation of the rooms. The process must also take future users into account, along with considering the natural environment and the social setting. The headquarters of Volkswohl Bund Versicherungen, completed in 2010 in Dortmund, is in this respect a stroke of luck for all involved: as general planner and consultant, TCHOBAN VOSS Architekten were able to design the building as a single piece. The company wanted a building that would convey its down-to-earth philosophy and integrate with the urban space in a way that is striking, without being modish or showy. The 17-storey high-rise at the edge of an urban block is modest - both inside and out - and responds to its location on all sides. In terms of height, the base is oriented on neighboring buildings and gives the urban development a well-defined edge. On the corner of the block the volume jumps back slightly, creating a small piazza and publicly accessible urban space, which, marked by paving consisting of strips of natural stone, leads inside through a multi-storey, gallery-lined entrance hall before flowing out again into an internal courtyard. The flat hierarchies of the insurance company are also reproduced in the exterior. The homogeneous façade structure of slender, dramatically vertical elements of natural stone expresses the similarity of all the office spaces and the democratic structure of the Volkswohl Bund.

THE BEGINNING OF THE 21ST CENTURY BROUGHT NOT JUST A NEW MILLENNIUM, BUT ALSO THE BEGINNING OF TWO MOVEMENTS THAT CHANGED EVERYTHING: THE DIGITAL AND THE ECOLOGICAL REVOLUTIONS.

The internal layout shows the serious consideration given to users needs. The design of the work area focuses on such things as communication and well-being. Two- and three-person rooms alternate with central lounge areas on each storey. Each office has ceiling-to-floor windows and thus not only abundant daylight, but also an attractive view of the urban surroundings. Good acoustics and a tranquil color scheme make for a pleasant and productive working environment. That this architecture elicits a positive response and is still effective even eight years after the building came into operation is indicated by its continuation in the second phase of the project, which is now under construction.

THE FUTURE THROUGH DIVERSITY

Most office buildings, however, are planned with no consideration for user structure; many companies forego their own company building for the sake of greater flexibility. In order to give future tenants the greatest possible freedom when devising layouts and workplace scenarios, a variable spatial concept is needed. This is the case with the office and company building at Große Bleichen 19 in Hamburg. Faced with enormous depth (80 meters, against a width of only 14 meters), TCHOBAN VOSS Architekten responded with a building volume in which lateral infrastructure cores and light wells enable flexible use of space and rapid adaptation to changing tenant requirements. The external spaces cut into the building ensure that all workspaces are properly illuminated and ventilated. The façade, whose bricks form a bridge to the adjacent listed old post-office building, also has large windows opening onto the natural surroundings, thereby increasing the amount of daylight.

The extension project for Kassenärztliche Vereinigung Sachsen (KVS) in Dresden, which was completed in 2015 to a design by TCHOBAN VOSS Architekten, also takes into account the need for flexibility and efficiency. It is the building's façade structure that provides the key to a variable layout. Its 1.35-meter-wide grid enables considerable flexibility in layout planning, which can be quickly adapted to new needs as they emerge in the future. By a barely perceptible variation of the

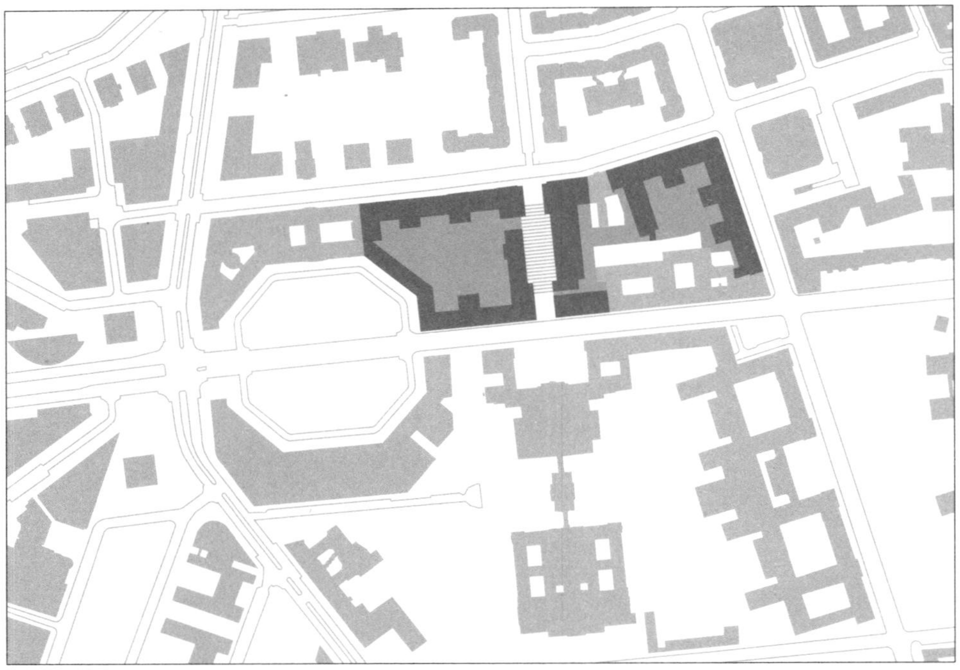

LP12 Mall of Berlin on Leipziger Platz was completed in the spring of 2014. In terms of urban planning, this architectural ensemble establishes a structural link between the shopping and entertainment area west of Potsdamer Platz and Friedrichstraße with its expensive shops.

window widths the architects have managed to subtly loosen the façade image, which in other respects is tranquil and harmonious, owing to its elements in natural stone. The tall windows help create workspaces with sufficient daylight and natural ventilation.

That an old building can also provide for such a diversity of needs is shown by the cloth factory renovated and extended by TCHOBAN VOSS Architekten in Berlin in 2016. Erected in 1966, this was originally an administration and storage building; today it contains numerous diverse offices and commercial spaces. The most striking intervention is the new façade design consisting of colorfully luminous printed bundles of thread that lie on top of the overall building envelope like an oversized woven structure. The pattern gives the building a new external identity. Inside, the architects have been more restrained, keeping the intervention in the existing structure to a minimum and thereby providing an example of the sustainable treatment of old buildings.

NATURAL SHOPPING EXPERIENCE

Advancing digitalization is also generating radical change in the world of shopping – and by extension in commercial architecture. In the near future the online shop will constitute the greater part of many companies' turnover. This, however, does not mean the end of shops in our downtown areas. Like office buildings, they are acquiring a prominent role as a social place with which clients associate emotions and stories. However, experience architecture alone is not sufficient: the retail trade is also developing an awareness of sustainability and atmosphere, among clients and sales staff alike. This means fairtrade clothes, bio shops, and local products on the one hand, and an atmosphere of wellbeing and references to the natural environment on the other.

TCHOBAN VOSS Architekten's design concept for Glacis Galerie, a shopping center with food court completed in 2015 in Neu-Ulm, has developed a model for shopping today based on consideration for urban planning: in the structure of the built-up area the complex is oriented on surrounding buildings while at the same time creating a new entrance to the city center. Two adjacent streets have been extended as glass galleries inside the building; this creates interesting visual axes, external links, and new flows of movement, bringing the environment back to life. Throughout the building, clients and employees are accompanied by natural daylight that enters the interior through large skylights. Light colors and high ceilings add to the friendly atmosphere.

Requirements regarding workplaces are changing. However, one important component has gained in significance: the workplace is and remains an integral part of our identity. To avoid threatening this status, the workplace has developed into a place for meetings, communication, and exchange. Freedom from rigid hierarchies calls for an open architecture that focuses on people. ■

VIEW OF THE FEDERAL ASSEMBLY BUILDING FROM THE GALLERY ON THE FIRST FLOOR OF LP 12 MALL OF BERLIN

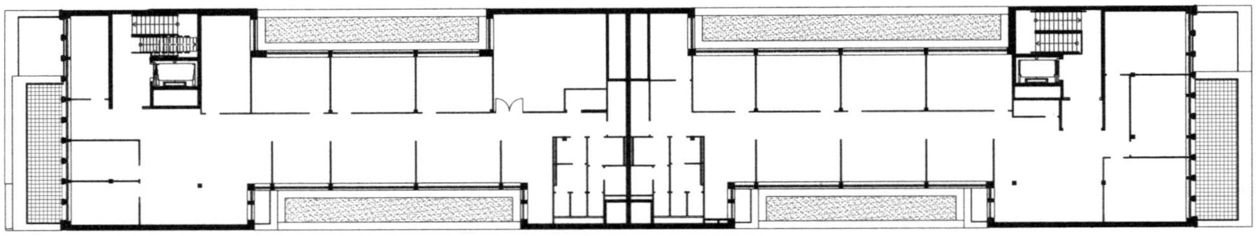

FLOOR PLAN. LEVEL 5

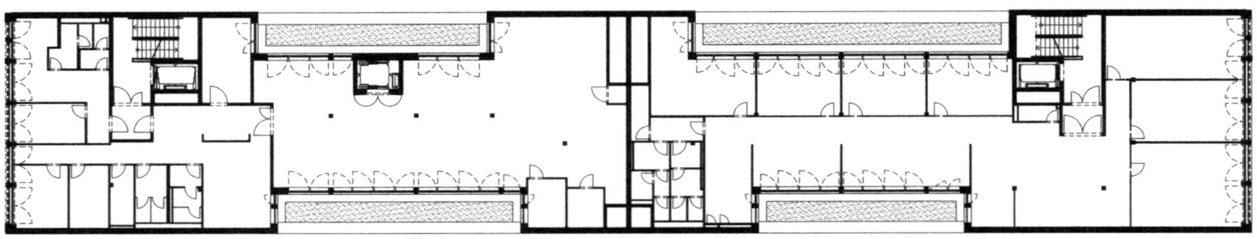

FLOOR PLAN. LEVEL 2

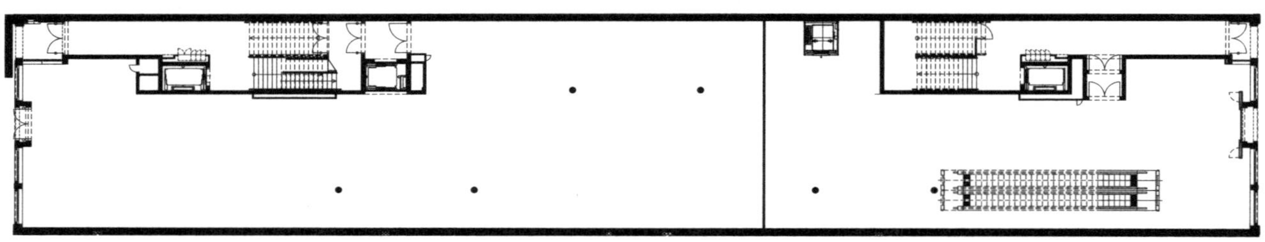

FLOOR PLAN. GROUND LEVEL

GROSSE BLEICHEN OFFICE AND BUSINESS BUILDING, HAMBURG

GALLERIA
GALLERIA
ALTE POST

MODERNIZATION AND CONVERSION OF A FORMER CLOTH FACTORY, BERLIN

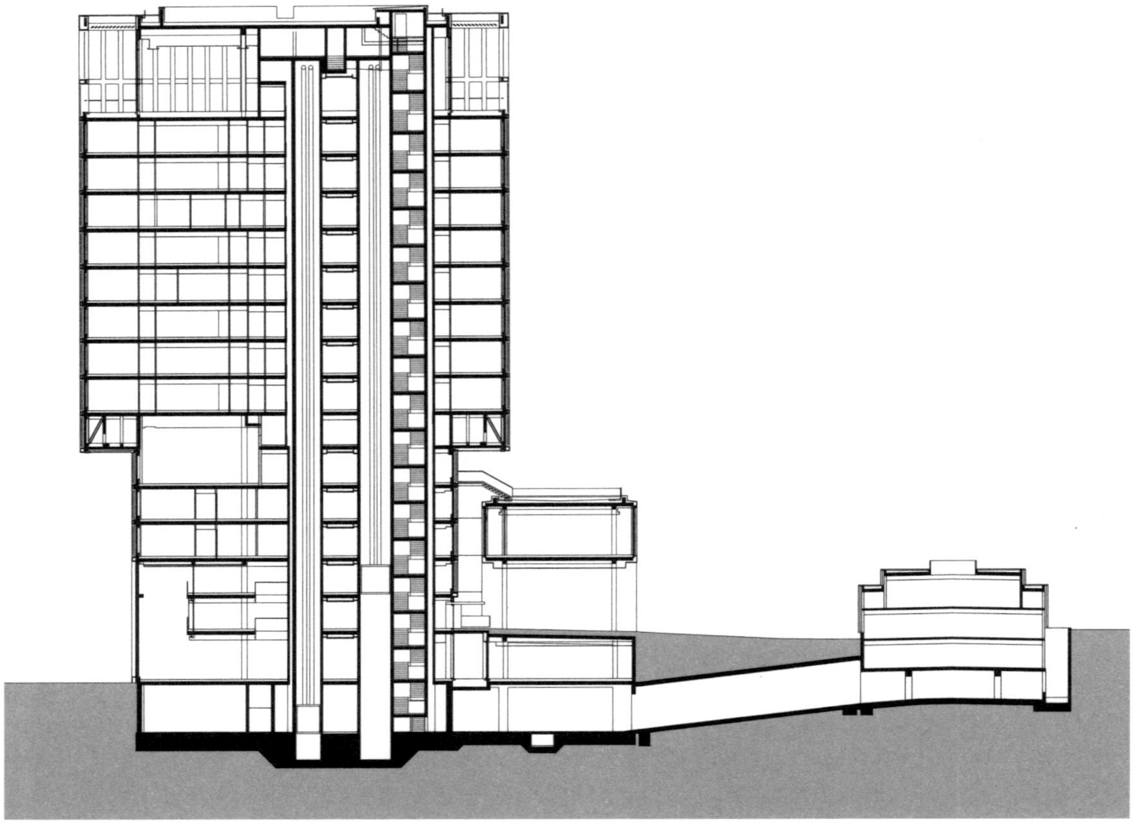

VOLKSWOHL BUND VERSICHERUNGEN, DORTMUND

VOLKSWOHL BUND

ASSOCIATION OF STATUTORY HEALTH INSURANCE PHYSICIANS KVS SACHSEN, DRESDEN

REPRESENTATIVES FOR EXISTING STRUCTURES

Handling existing buildings is an increasingly large and complex part of an architect's work. Each project requires an individual approach which takes into account specific conditions and an array of parameters. Here we look at four projects by TCHOBAN VOSS Architekten, ranging from modern extensions and modest updates to sensitive renovations.

BY LUISE RELLENSMANN

Conversion, alteration, modernization, and reutilization: the building industry has always been shaped by development of existing structures. The idea of the architect as someone who designs buildings as if nothing existed prior, has nonetheless endured. Today many architects' daily work is in fact a matter of transformation rather than demolition: two-thirds of current construction activity involves existing buildings. In addition to preserving a building's cultural qualities, this is also a question of sustainability and grey energy. Architectural design involving existing structures – and not just in the case of listed buildings – is a special focus in TCHOBAN VOSS Architekten's daily work. The firm's projects show how reconstruction can be an attractive design task.

> ’DEVELOPMENT IS ALWAYS BETTER THAN DEMOLITION.
>
> TCHOBAN VOSS ARCHITEKTEN

The massive building of the former "palace of justice" in the Sudenburg district of Magdeburg lost its imposing middle part, almost-50-meter-high corner tower, and north wing when it was bombed by the Allies in 1945. However, the now-listed remaining fragment of the originally symmetrical four-wing court complex retains an impressive radiance. Designing buildings for the judiciary was, when this palace of justice was built between 1900 and 1906, still a new kind of brief; before this, the judiciary had not really had a space of its own. This four-storey building with its historicist façade of natural stone was part of the Prussian program for construction of court buildings, the first embodiment of the principle of separation of powers in architectural form.

With its ongoing reconstruction and renovation of the listed wing TCHOBAN VOSS Architekten is consolidating the Magdeburg District Court in its historical spaces and thus further developing the building's original use. This continuity of use meant that only very limited intervention in the building's fabric was required. The dimensions of the rooms remain unchanged: the size of the old court rooms makes them suitable for use as modern offices; and the comfortably-high waiting rooms and chambers lend themselves to a variety of uses. Even after more than a century, the essential structures continue to be usable without major changes. The architects from TCHOBAN VOSS Architekten's Dresden office had to pull off a few tricks to put lifts in the spandrel – thus creating accessibility without the need for additional built structure.

A CULTURE OF DEVELOPMENT OF EXISTING BUILDINGS

This project shows how TCHOBAN VOSS Architekten practises a culture of development of existing buildings that goes beyond conservation requirements to encompass concern for grey energy and conservation of architectural strata. The plans include renovation of the new wing that was erected in 2001 on the site of the part of the building destroyed in the war and optimize links between the old and new parts of the building.

Whereas many architects feel constricted when reconstructing existing buildings, the leading architect on this project, who since the 1990s has specialized in reconstruction of historical buildings, is, on the contrary, inspired by the diverse conditions found in historical buildings. "The design task is," says Bettina Kempe-Gebert, "to bring everything together, to find a coherent solution for all the requirements in thecontext of preserving a building and developing it further. To preserve a piece of modern history in a time of ever more rapid change in construction culture is what motivates Kempe-Gebert in her work. She is convinced that this "palace of justice," which was for its time a pioneer in terms of construction technology, is something special. The imposing building's historical envelope conceals innovative construction technology that during the course of renovation has remained legible in the rounded edges of the conical coving. The interiors were renovated in accordance with the color scheme of around 1900.

"At the district court building a sensitive renovation is taking place through the unobtrusive addition of missing functions – a project that demands a certain modesty of the architects," sums up Jörg Rudloff, associate partner and reconstruction expert at TCHOBAN VOSS Architekten's Dresden branch. For many architects, however, the design process is only exciting when it is a matter of adding a new, visible layer of time. Listed buildings have always been reconstructed; it is how they prove their viability. Making a positive contribution to the survival of a listed building is what Jörg Rudloff finds attractive in reconstruction work.

> ,IN A TIME OF EVER MORE RAPIDLY CHANGING CONSTRUCTION CULTURE IT IS RIGHT TO PRESERVE A PIECE OF MODERN HISTORY.
>
> BETTINA KEMPE-GEBERT

SETTING UP AND ARRANGING

A project which is exemplary of this approach is the renovation and extension of Schloss Sonnenstein in Pirna to accommodate the district administration for Saxonian Switzerland/Osterzgebirge, a project which was completed in 2011. The fortress goes back to the 13th century and can be found in paintings by Canaletto. This is a spot whose history includes many changes and terrible events, especially in its more recent past. The future seat of the local administration was converted for use as a sanatorium in the 18th century and under Nationalist Socialism was used as a killing center. Thousands were murdered here during the Nazis' euthanasia program – crimes that are commemorated by a memorial in the castle's Elbe wing. In the DDR period the aviation industry used the building to develop and manufacture jet engines.

The wing of the castle complex converted by TCHOBAN VOSS Architekten had been unoccupied since the 1980s. Trees were running wild in the partially ruined walls, which were on the point of falling down the slope of the castle hill. The renovation and fundamental reconstruction involved expanding the internal spaces for use as modern offices. In order to keep the additions as slight as possible, the architects opted to decant the district administration's large departments such as the vehicle-registration office and the cafeteria. For this purpose they devised not a free-standing building, but small additional blocks, which set up and rearrange the entrance area, weaving this complex of buildings together to form a coherent whole.

Built as a pavilion on a socle storey, the cafeteria plays an important role in the layout of the Sonnenstein complex, serving as a link between the different structures. Overall, the design of the site has given it greater clarity of image and development, explains Rudloff. The new block takes up the rhythm of the castle façade and is distantly reminiscent of a cloister. In order that the new concrete buildings should not contrast too greatly with the old fortress, the architects chose a sand color as an echo of the Saxonian sandstone. The additions remain legible even without any perceptible change in color and materials.

IN HARMONY WITH CONSERVATION REQUIREMENTS

In converting and developing the Hamburger Hof in the center of Berlin TCHOBAN VOSS Architekten opted for contrast. "Clear legibility by means of hard transitions" is how Frederik-Sebastian Scholz, the associate partner responsible for this project, describes the concept behind this design. To the historical, plaster-and brick-courtyards, which had been expanded over the course of two centuries, the architects have added diverse roof structures and a new block in glass and metal. Formally, the latter, with its overhanging penthouse storey, forms the greatest contrast with the existing buildings. However, like the added roof shapes, the new block adopts the footprint of previously existing buildings, ensuring the survival of the courtyard's mature structure.

The apparently contrasting choice of materials is, in the final analysis, a logical continuation of the typical way of constructing an industrial courtyard, given that the successively larger historical extensions of the front part of the building, which was erected in 1828, were all carried out with an eye to saving money. Accordingly, the new additions have been designed to be equally cost-effective – using industrial glass and sheet-metal façades made from prefabricated elements. At the back, the complex ends at Krausnick Park, a public green space. In expanding the structure, the architects have deliberately left the park-facing brick façade (on the other side of which are new apartments) as it is; the façade's visible division into parts tells the story of at least four phases of construction.

> ’THE GREATEST CHALLENGE IS IMPLEMENTING STATUTORY CONSTRUCTION STANDARDS – ABOVE ALL, FIRE-SAFETY PRECAUTIONS – IN HARMONY WITH CONSERVATION REQUIREMENTS.
>
> FREDERIK-SEBASTIAN SCHOLZ

The Hamburger Hof is situated in the Spandauer Vorstadt, Berlin's largest and best-preserved historical district. Famous or even infamous initially in the 1990s for its clubs, this neighborhood has developed into a residential and business area and hip district that is attractive to tourists and home to numerous well-renovated buildings. The vaulted cellar of the business courtyard in Hamburgerstraße was once a place where people danced. Over the course of renovation the underground passageways were dug deeper, the cellars were joined together, and related spatial concepts were developed from their former uses as bowling alleys and music clubs. Today the Hamburger Hof offers not off-the-peg offices, but unconventional spaces for creative types and agencies. In order to preserve a long-established carpentry shop in the inner courtyard, the architects elegantly incorporated noise-control systems into the existing building, in consultation with the conservation authorities. Scholz sees the greatest challenge as implementing statutory construction standards – above all, fire-safety precautions – in harmony with conservation requirements.

CLARIFY AND UPDATE

A different kind of restoration project involving reconstruction and the addition of a new storey has been realized by TCHOBAN VOSS Architekten not far from the Tiergarten in Berlin on Straße des 17. Juni. Ernst-Reuter-Haus – formerly the seat of the German Association of Cities – has since 2012 housed the Federal Office for Building and Regional Planning. The design of the building is based on Albert Speer's plans for Germania, Hitler's world capital. This administrative building is the only design for Germania's East-West Axis that was realized. Although construction began in the late 1930s, it was not completed during the war. Only the side wing and the shell of a middle part existed when in the early 1950s contributions by various communities from the Association of German Cities enabled completion of the work. The glazed coats of arms in the courtyard-facing window of the building's imposing staircase recall these contributions. The post-war renovation saw the building's exterior completed in the Neoclassical style; when visitors enter the lobby, however, they find interior design from the 1950s with brass doors and columns clad with tessellation. It is this contrast which TCHOBAN VOSS Architekten have conspicuously developed further in their conservation-oriented renovation. At the beginning of the project the architects discovered a foyer area that had been reshaped a number of times over the years. Under a layer of caramel-brown plaster they were able to expose black mosaic with colored bands and sprinkles of gold. "95 percent of the original decoration had survived," enthuses Philipp Bauer, the partner responsible for this project. "All we had to do was add small pieces in places to complete it."

Bauer describes the design concept for the office as "clarifying and updating." This is an approach that can be seen especially clearly in the 700-square-meter lobby, the building's hub and fulcrum. The foyer has been substantially renovated, somewhat cleaned up, and slightly added to. To create flowing transitions and stronger connections between inner and outer space, a massive wall in the vestibule has disappeared. The intarsia work that was attached to it - an armorial wall with the coats of arms of cities in central and eastern Germany, from the time of Germany's division into two countries - has been moved to the second floor. Glass railings in place of masonry banisters ensure greater transparency, while the addition of luminous ceilings has joined the parts of the foyer together into a spatial unit. The result is an architecture whose additions continue the existing design instead of contrasting with it.

These examples from the work of TCHOBAN VOSS Architekten show that there can be no single strategy when working with existing buildings. As a rule, listed buildings possess qualities that the firm's architects want to preserve. It is part of TCHOBAN VOSS Architekten's corporate culture to engage with municipal authorities in dialogue with conservation authorities at the earliest possible moment regarding consultation structures and standards of quality. The conservation authorities are not opponents, but strong allies. However, even outside the context of listed buildings, TCHOBAN VOSS Architekten's principle is: development is always better than demolition. The firm works with each client to develop a list of aims so as to find joint solutions that are consistent with the existing qualities of a building. In this TCHOBAN VOSS Architekten always views itself as a respectful spokesman for the existing structures. The priority is preservation of a building's basic fabric. ■

The Magdeburg District Court has remained in the rooms it has always occupied. This continuity of use made it possible to keep intervention in the building's fabric to a minimum.

MAGDEBURG REGIONAL COURT HOUSE

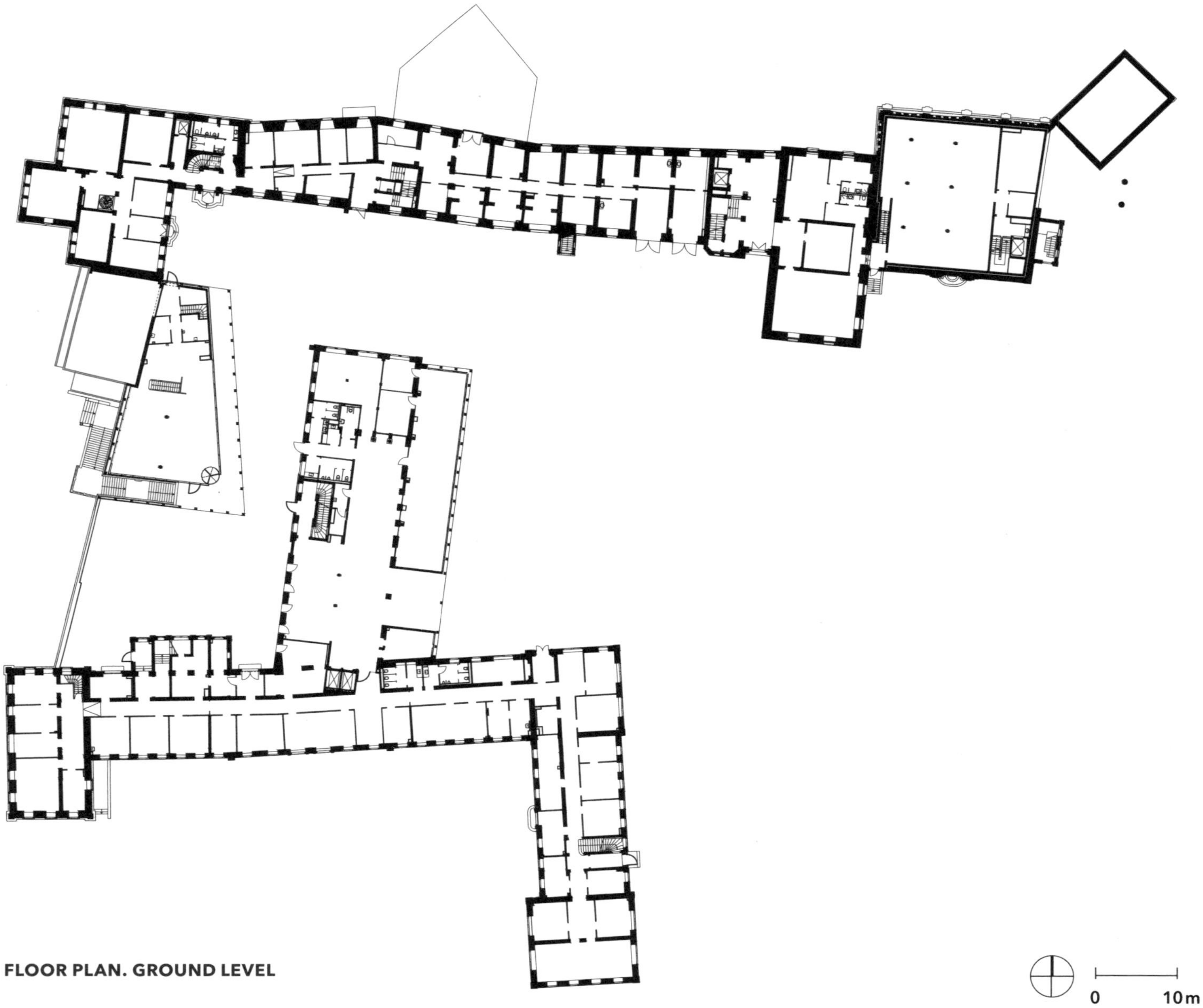

FLOOR PLAN. GROUND LEVEL

SCHLOSS SONNENSTEIN, PIRNA

ERNST-REUTER-HAUS, BERLIN

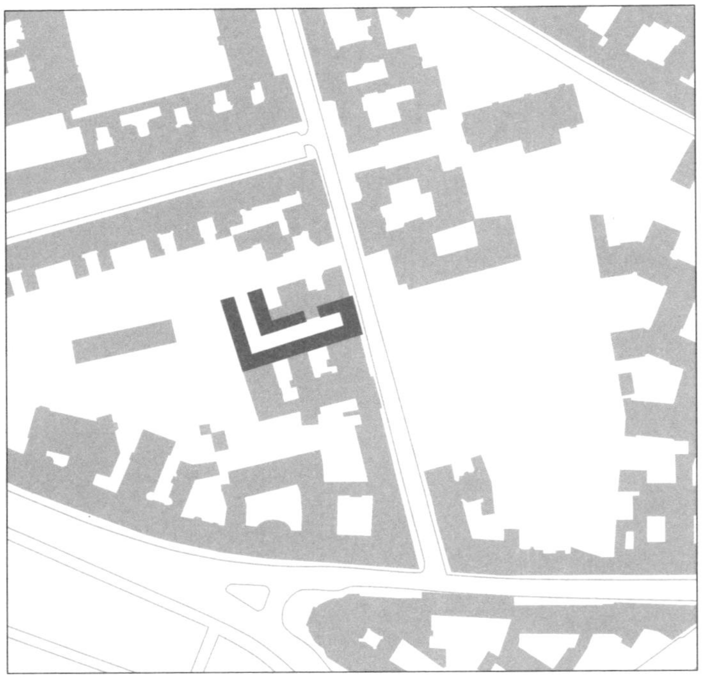

SECTION AA

0 10m

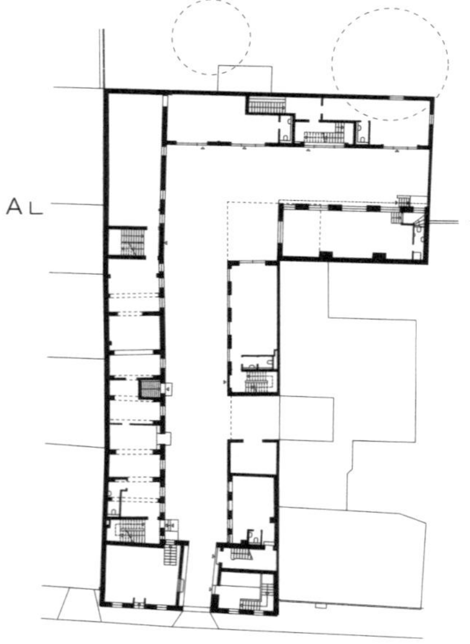

FLOOR PLAN. GROUND LEVEL

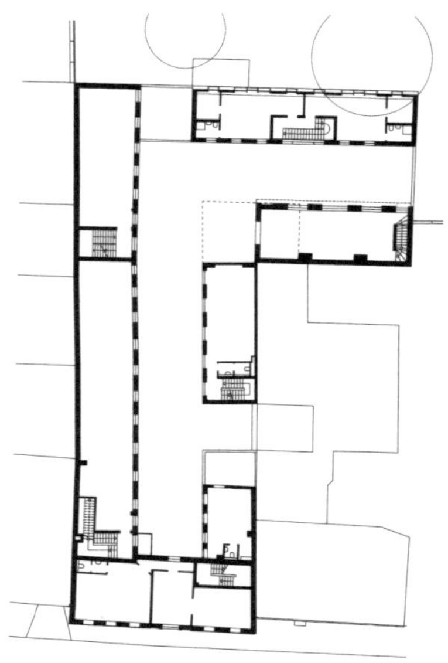

FLOOR PLAN. LEVEL 1

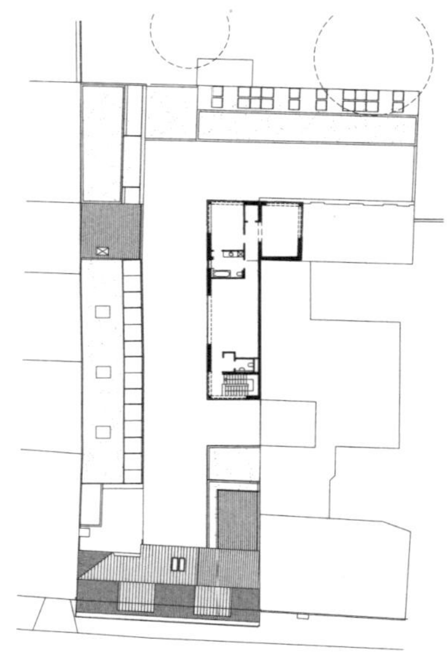

FLOOR PLAN. LEVEL 4

HAMBURGER HOF ON GROSSE HAMBURGER STRASSE, BERLIN

0 10m

COME TO STAY

TCHOBAN VOSS ARCHITEKTEN BUILD HOTELS IN URBAN CENTERS

BY JASMIN JOUHAR

Berlin, the main railway station. In just a few years the area around this new transport hub has been transformed from a no man's land into a bustling metropolitan district. Every day the infrastructure brings hundreds of thousands of people here by train, U-bahn, and tram. Most of the travellers are here for only a short time, to change trains, make purchases, or buy a snack. Some, however, stay overnight since an urban hub such as a railway station naturally includes hotels. In the 19th century, when the railway with its large station buildings blazed a trail into cities, the process launched rapid urban growth. Hotels from this epoch often looked like palaces and with their splendid façades and beautiful lobbies were meeting points for fine society.

The castle as architectonic model has long since had its day, but hotels have retained their status as half-public urban spaces. Most recently, they have even gained in importance – as temporary workspaces for a mobile generation that always carries its office with it on smartphones or laptops. The new inner-city hotels often see themselves, quite understandably, as places in which visitors and locals can come together. It remains important to ask: how should hotel buildings present themselves in urban centers? Five projects by TCHOBAN VOSS Architekten from the past ten years exhibit the entire range of urban and architectonic variations possible in a large city today.

> ’OUR CONCERN WAS TO DIFFERENTIATE THE TWO BUILDINGS: THEY NEED TO REINFORCE ONE ANOTHER.
>
> ULRIKE GRAEFENHAIN

ARCHITECTURE OF CONTINUITY

In sight of Berlin's main railway station, on the northeast side of Europaplatz, a building with a façade in light-colored brick marks with absolute self-assurance the corner of the square. Completed in 2015, the new hotel building by TCHOBAN VOSS Architekten mediates between the railway station, the new Europa block, and the neighborhood around the Hamburger Bahnhof Museum. It houses two hotels belonging to two different categories – an IBIS in the west wing and the Amano Grand Central in the east wing. The cubic structure stands at the edge of a street block, its two principal façades – on Invalidenstraße and Heidestraße – positioned adjacent to one another across the corner. A canopy further emphasizes the corner and leads to the main entrance of the Amano Hotel in Heidestraße. The vertical windows with their dark profiles, the light ochre color of the bricks, and the tranquil structure are all references to old buildings in the vicinity. The façade stands out for its depth; the window surrounds are doubly stepped, creating excitement and contrast in these areas. Here TCHOBAN VOSS Architekten has realized an architecture of continuity that does not set out to stand out as new at any price, but reiterates the vision of Berlin as a city of stone.

IN THE SPIRIT OF THE MODERN

Also in the immediate vicinity of a railway station is the hotel at Nordkopf in Wolfsburg, completed in 2014. This building stands south of the railway station and the Mittellandkanal. On the other side of the canal is the enormous Volkswagen factory with its Autostadt ("Car City"). If the 19th century city was the reference point for the double hotel in Berlin, for Wolfsburg TCHOBAN VOSS Architekten infused their design with the spirit of Modernism. The building for Meliá Group (Spain) is a sweeping gesture connecting the railway station's southern entrance with the downtown area. The horizontally layered façades with striking, continuous bands convey something of Modernism's fascination with movement and speed, airplanes, cruise liners, and, last but not least, the automobile. This is an apt association given the proximity of the Volkswagen factory, and it is one that is also functionally integrated. Through its recessed ground floor the building forms a continuous, protected space leading to the forecourt. This passageway zone looks like an invitation extended by the hotel to the city.

SUBTLE GRID

'The urban traveller's home' is how the Meininger hotel chain promotes its buildings – a hybrid of hostel and hotel combining comfort with low room prices. Meininger's target market is predominantly a young international clientele. The hotel "Berlin East Side Gallery", which was designed by TCHOBAN VOSS Architekten, scores well with young 'urban travellers', but not just for its prominent location in a cultural hotspot in Berlin's Friedrichshain district; numerous Internet reviews describe the building as "stylish and modern". Completed in 2017, it has a floor area of approximately 7280 square meters and a total of 245 rooms.

Directly opposite the hotel is the East Side Gallery, which with its street art on the longest surviving stretch of the Berlin wall is one of the German capital's tourist magnets. The city block between the Ostbahnhof and the Mercedes-Benz Arena has in recent years, however, also become a rapidly growing location for offices and services. A free-standing structure with its 36-meter-high 10-storey tower, the Meininger Hotel is self-confident in posture, but without dominating its urban surroundings. The restrained, yet varied façade structures the building and imparts visual variety. As with numerous other hotels they have designed, TCHOBAN VOSS Architekten here opted for natural stone, cladding the external envelope with limestone from the second floor upwards. The façade grid is formed vertically by fluted pilasters, each of which stretches over two storeys. The irregular positioning of the floor-to-ceiling, slender windows creates an impression of variety. Horizontally, the hotel building is structured by continuous bands on each storey.

> ' THE FAÇADE ADOPTS THE STRUCTURE OF THE WILHELMINE ERA IN ITS RHYTHM AND ARTICULATION.
>
> FREDERIK-SEBASTIAN SCHOLZ

The design concept and choice of materials, wrote the online magazine BauNetz on the hotel's opening, convey "a surprisingly high-class impression for accommodation in the lower price band." In the minds of younger users the façade grid may arouse other associations: in the opinion of Meininger Group's online editors, the façade would "make for a super Tetris game."

URBAN LANDMARK

In another hotel project TCHOBAN VOSS Architekten were able to develop a metropolitan character even more strongly. The Meliá Hotel in Düsseldorf, which opened in 2009, makes good use of its prominent urban position on the northern part of the Hofgarten, the city's central park, transitioning from perimeter block development into an imposing tower on the corner of the street block. The architects were able to build high, up to eleven storeys. The location, directly opposite the Hofgarten, near Düsseldorf's historical center, made it possible to create an urban landmark that would be visible from afar – a stand-alone building that at the same time, thanks to its uncluttered façade structure and cladding of light-colored natural stone, makes a good fit with its surroundings. The lower parts of the building are of five and seven storeys, taking their height from the adjacent buildings. The partially recessed block forms a small forecourt, thus additionally emphasizing the corner. Other distinctive features of this project are the imposing ground floor and an implied mezzanine; additionally, every two storeys are coupled together in a unifying frame. These echoes of a colossal, classical order impart a metropolitan feel to the 200-room building – a contemporary echo of the splendor of the old metropolitan hotels.

UNOBTRUSIVE ORNAMENTATION

The location of the Titanic Hotel in Berlin may not stand out. This 389-room hotel is on Chausseestraße in the city's Mitte district. Diagonally across from it is the mighty complex of the Federal Intelligence Service (BND). The environs here are shaped by a colorful mix of office and residential buildings deriving from a range of periods from the Wilhelmine age through the Modernism of the DDR to the present day. "This plot of land was difficult to plan," says Frederik-Sebastian Scholz, the associate partner responsible for this project. "It was one of a large number of empty plots in perimeter-based block development from the Wilhelmine period. A very jagged urban setting." But this location is unquestionably one thing: urban. The street block has a lively appearance, with lots going on, including cafes, restaurants, shops, and supermarkets to attract the public. In this heterogeneous environment TCHOBAN VOSS Architekten set out to establish a haven of peace. This is why the new hotel building is so ordered and symmetrical; it needed to avoid at all costs looking agitated. The extensive street-facing façade of white precast concrete consists of three parts: a slightly set-back middle part is flanked by two lateral risalti, which align with the block edge. "The façade adopts the structure of the Wilhelmine era in its rhythm and articulation," explains Frederik-Sebastian Scholz. Together, the elements form a tectonic structure and frame the vertical windows. A striking feature is the canopy, which is positioned in front of the middle part of the façade and protects the entrances to the hotel and the external restaurant. Additionally, it creates a space in front of the hotel and connects inside and outside, making it a truly distinctive feature.

For all its orderliness, the hotel building is in no way lacking in energy. Even if the façade is tranquil and harmonious, interesting details come to light when you look more closely, such as the subtle ornamentation that covers one part of the façade panels. The client is from a Berlin family of Turkish origin that started off in catering and is now active in the hotel industry. The abstract ornaments based on the circle were designed by Sergei Tchoban, helped by graphic designers from TCHOBAN VOSS Architekten, specially for this building. The ornament is based on classic Turkish ornaments such as you might find in Istanbul, for instance. Molds were used to cast the pattern in concrete. The other façade panels are also of the same high-quality architectural concrete, which is partly completely smooth and partly grit-blasted. "We developed the concrete ourselves," says Frederik-Sebastian Scholz. "It's pure white, with the addition of special aggregates such as white sand. Instead of shingle or gravel, we used ground quartz. This gives the façade a special lustre and sparkle." The building has a material quality that ages beautifully and is likely to generate a patina.

Whether in Berlin, Wolfsburg, or Düsseldorf, TCHOBAN VOSS Architekten's hotel buildings stand for a contemporary treatment of the city. They claim their place in the urban fabric while making diverse urban-planning and historical references and addressing themselves to public space. These are not impersonal transit stations; the consideration they give to quality in every detail means that they represent an architecture that has come to stay. ■

A clear and strong reticular structure: only at second glance does the façade reveal the slight movement which has been achieved by shifting the windows and recessing the mouldings.

HOTELS AT HAUPTBAHNHOF, BERLIN

FLOOR PLAN. TYPICAL FLOOR

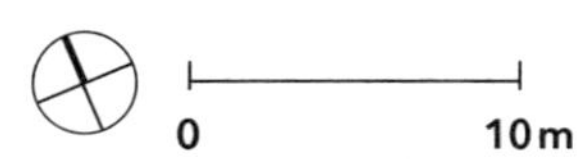

HOTEL AM NORDKOPF, WOLFSBURG

MEININGER HOTEL AT POSTBAHNHOF, BERLIN

MEININGER M HOTEL
MEININGER M HOTEL

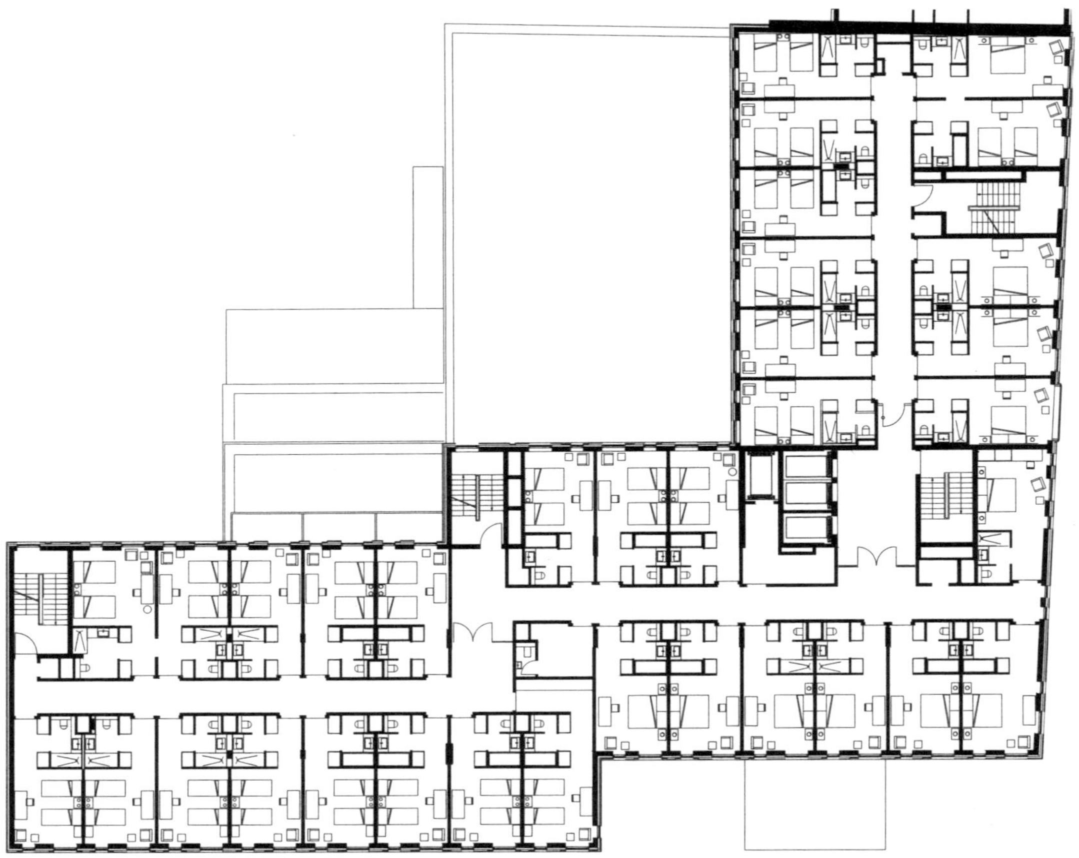

FLOOR PLAN. TYPICAL FLOOR

MELIÁ HOTEL, DÜSSELDORF

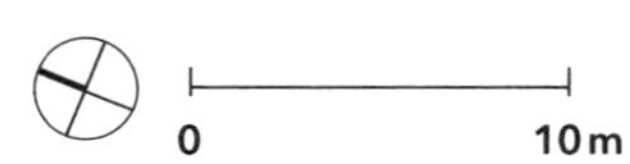

MELIÃ DÜSSELDORF

TITANIC HOTEL, BERLIN

QUALITY COUNTS!

A SURVEY OF RESIDENTIAL DEVELOPMENT IN FOUR CITIES

BY CHRISTINA GRÄWE

Residential development has been a big theme in recent years, and will be in years to come, for planners and increasingly for politicians too. Finding residential space means wrestling with price per square meter, quality standards, building approvals, and energy issues. If you have an old rental agreement or became an owner at the right time, you can count yourself lucky. Everyone else is hoping for a rapid increase in supply of housing, including through activation of long-neglected capacity. Residential development is an important part of TCHOBAN VOSS Architekten's portfolio. The firm's residential projects are diverse and are to be found in very different locations and situations.

(West) Berlin, summer 1988: clusters of people form in front of newspaper kiosks, the sports and culture sections fluttering to the ground so that the real-estate section can be studied more thoroughly. Shortly afterwards: clusters of people form in front of phone boxes. The next day, the interested parties form a line stretching from the ground floor to the apartment on the fifth.

Berlin, summer 2018: apartment advertisements are now researched on the Internet, the mobile phone has replaced the phone kiosk. Arriving at the address you were looking for, it's like being taken back about 30 years: there are people on top of people, all the way from the ground floor to the fifth.

The situation is the same in all conurbations where people are drawn by workplaces, universities, infrastructure, the anonymity of a large city, or the romantic atmosphere of a kiez (local neighborhood). "Nothing has really changed in living patterns during the last 100 years," says Sergei Tchoban. He means three things: the high proportion of renters in Germany, the fact that households are predominantly settled in one place, and the return to the communal thinking of the 1920s. Politicians have declared housing a top priority. The "Alliance for Affordable Housing" has existed since summer 2014. Four years later, a housing summit took place at the federal chancellery; at the same time, an alternative housing summit was held by social and tenants' associations, organizations that felt under-represented and criticize the government for being too investor-friendly. Of the 1.5 million apartments that are supposedly to be created by 2021, a mere 280 000 were built in 2017. For the period between January and July 2018 the Federal Statistical Office registered a growth of 1.9 percent in building permits compared to the same period in the year before. The figures show that things are moving; reality shows that they are moving too slowly. And it may justifiably be asked whether volumes of housing construction are sufficient in those situations where there is the greatest need, namely for households with low incomes and increasingly for those with average incomes as well. No: many planners note that land prices are too high for this. As Sergei Tchoban observes with frustration, architects have no influence on investors' games such as multiple salesthat reduce the budget for construction itself: "There must be the political will to put a brake on speculation," he notes. Construction too is becoming ever more expensive. However, TCHOBAN VOSS Architekten is determined to maintain its quality standards. This goes for both individual houses and the impact that architects inevitably have on the built environment. With this responsibility in mind, Ekkehard Voss takes the view that "solidity, timelessness, and urban integration" should be fundamental considerations for every design project. The diversity of challenges faced by the architects and the diversity of ways in which they handle these challenges is shown by a survey of the firm's projects in Hamburg, Ludwigsfelde, Kleve, and Berlin.

DENSIFICATION IN LARGE CITIES: HAMBURG-LOKSTEDT

One of the key terms heard repeatedly in the national debate about construction is densification, whether by means of new construction or the building on of additional storeys. In Lokstedt, a growing district in the center of Hamburg, densification is taking the form of construction of a new neighborhood on the boundary with Eppendorf. Situated on a 4.8-hectare piece of land that used to belong to a civil-engineering company, the neighborhood that has sprung up is mainly made up of apartment blocks and is being built in several stages with almost 380 one-level apartments in all. The program also includes subsidized and student apartments as well as a public park with which the clients would like to extend the green character of the neighborhood. TCHOBAN VOSS Architekten, which took third place in the design competition involving seven invited participants, was assigned 130 apartments. Its 12 three- and four-storey houses were ready for occupation in spring 2018. All the participating architects agreed to a design code specifying green roofs and façades of light-colored brick. The first stage also incorporated construction of a combined heat and power station catering for the entire settlement – since the clients wanted a sustainable energy concept as well as extensive provisions for barrier-free access to the apartments. Students will probably have to wait a little for construction of the student accommodation, says project manager Beate Schonlau, since the publically-funded apartments in this first construction stage are intended for families.

What is being built at Lockstedt are solid, timeless houses that make a good fit with the existing urban structure. Ekkehard Voss calls this "vibrancy, not uncontrolled growth" and makes the case for this to be achieved using architecture that shows "composure, not attitude." Voss's overall principle is: "We need thorough mixing and diversity". Does this provide a comprehensive answer to the pressing need? And what is the situation with modular construction? Ekkehard Voss sees the latter as involving the risk of monotony and loss of quality. "Good examples, whether built using prefabrication or conventional means, need to be published much more widely in order to provide role models."

" SOLIDITY, TIMELESSNESS, AND INTEGRATION IN THE STRUCTURE OF THE CITY ARE AMONG THE FUNDAMENTAL CONSIDERATIONS FOR EVERY DESIGN PROJECT.

EKKEHARD VOSS

DENSIFICATION IN THE CITY CENTER: LUDWIGSFELDE

"Potsdamer Straße is glazed all the way to the railway station ... Sometimes, for all the glass, you no longer know whether you are standing in front of a house or have already entered it," writes Antje Rávic Strubel in her novel Tupolev 134 (published in 2004) of the new architecture in her home town, Ludwigsfelde in Brandenburg. She could not, however, have had in mind the three buildings erected by TCHOBAN VOSS Architekten in 2018 on a parallel street, Clara-Zetkin-Straße. These have socle storeys clad in brick, upper storeys plastered in a light color, and ceiling-to-floor windows. They densify a settlement of row houses built in the 1970s to 1990s. For the clients, Ludwigsfelder Wohnungsbaugenossenschaft ('Ludwigsfelde Housing-Construction Cooperative'), the new ensemble was its first new construction project since the Berlin wall came down.

Arranged like the sails of windmills around a car-free, green courtyard, the three-storey new buildings form a free-standing group of houses without disturbing the existing spatial structure. The buildings are very compact, resulting in more residential space than expected. In spite of the depth of the buildings, the bathrooms still receive daylight. All the apartments have access to outside ground-level terraces or large balconies; the roof terraces are especially attractive, due to the setback on this storey. In the terms set for the ideas competition for this development, the accents placed by LWG were already clear: for Henry Suczawski, the chairman of the board, it was important that the housing should be functional and barrier-free. Another requirement was the use of good materials – "high-quality, no luxury" – in a range of timeless colors. "All that has come off very well," comments Henry Suczawski. "Very harmoniously." He has gotten "what the visualizations promised." For his part, Ekkehard Voss is also happy that the designs have been realized as originally conceived. He and his associate partner, Jörg Rudloff, feel that the way the cooperative identifies closely with its buildings and the high degree of loyalty among the tenants are good omens for further collaboration. Consideration is already being given to a follow-up project.

FURTHER DEVELOPMENT IN KLEVE

In Kleve the district, the starting point, and the brief were all different. This city with a population of 50 000 has since 2009 been home to the headquarters of Rhine-Waal University of Applied Sciences; the new campus, also designed by TCHOBAN VOSS Architekten, was completed in 2012. Student numbers are continuously growing. On the eastern side of the Spoy Canal a residence hall for 112 was finished at the end of 2013. Situated on the northern end of the campus, it marks an end point for the latter's development. The building consists of two blocks - one four storeys high; the other, five - linked by fully glazed passageways. The colors and materials of the blocks, which are clad in fine-grained white plaster, refer to other buildings on the campus. The client did not want to enclose the space with fences; the grill area, seating areas, and canal embankment are accessible to the public, and there are also spaces for bicycles. The two buildings have been assigned different colors, a differentiation that is adumbrated in the modest external building numbers and then continued inside in the colored floors and wall panels. The dot pattern was taken from the glittering waters of the canal; the same pattern decorates the lower third of the glass parapets in front of the floor-to-ceiling windows. The bathrooms are prefabricated units in shades of grey and tomato-red, with cast-resin floors and HPL plastic panels on the walls and ceilings - with its glass shower walls and shelves, it is a robust and at the same time sophisticated design. Generous consideration has also been given to single residents, who pay between 260 and 280 euros for 25 square meters in a single apartment or a two- to three-room shared apartment. Dierk Schafmeyer, an associate partner, explains that the complex is designed to be converted to conventional accommodation should student numbers decline. Also important was the energy concept, which meets the passive-house standard, thereby securing this project's inclusion in the "100 climate-protected settlements in North Rhine-Westphalia" publicly funded program for 2011.

> ' GOOD CRAFTSMANSHIP MUST BE VALUED MORE HIGHLY: QUALITY COUNTS!
>
> SERGEI TCHOBAN

DENSIFICATION IN THE CAPITAL: BERLIN MITTE

In Berlin's most popular neighborhoods demand for densification is particularly high. A vacant lot in the Mitte district in the city center was filled by a combined apartment building and business center in 2016. The apartments from the second floor upwards have floor areas of between 70 and 90 square meters; the 290-square-meters glazed penthouse occupies the entire setback storey, including the roof terrace. There is another terrace on the one-storey block that extends into the garden. The remaining apartments all have deep loggias. The building's proportions make it a good fit with its surroundings. At the same time, this is a very conspicuous edifice. The white concrete elements that frame all the apertures give them the appearance of peep-boxes integrated into the façade. The same approach has been taken to the two-storey-high building door. This emphasis extends over three sides of the building. For all the cleanness of craftsmanship, this might appear lacking in refinement were it not for the playfulness present in the arrangement of the recumbent and vertical windows and were it not embedded in a fine façade of iridescent bricks of an ochre-sand color.

Is this the kind of living space that is now so urgently needed? Sergei Tchoban finds the prices per square meter required for high-quality construction excessive. However, architects have as little influence on this as they do on speculation on plots of land. "They have to respond to the market," comments Tchoban. Whether in Hamburg, Ludwigsfelde, Kleve, or Berlin, quality craftsmanship is in demand. The architects' plea is that "Good craftsmanship must be valued more highly: quality counts!" ■

STUDENT RESIDENCE ON BRIENER STRASSE, KLEVE

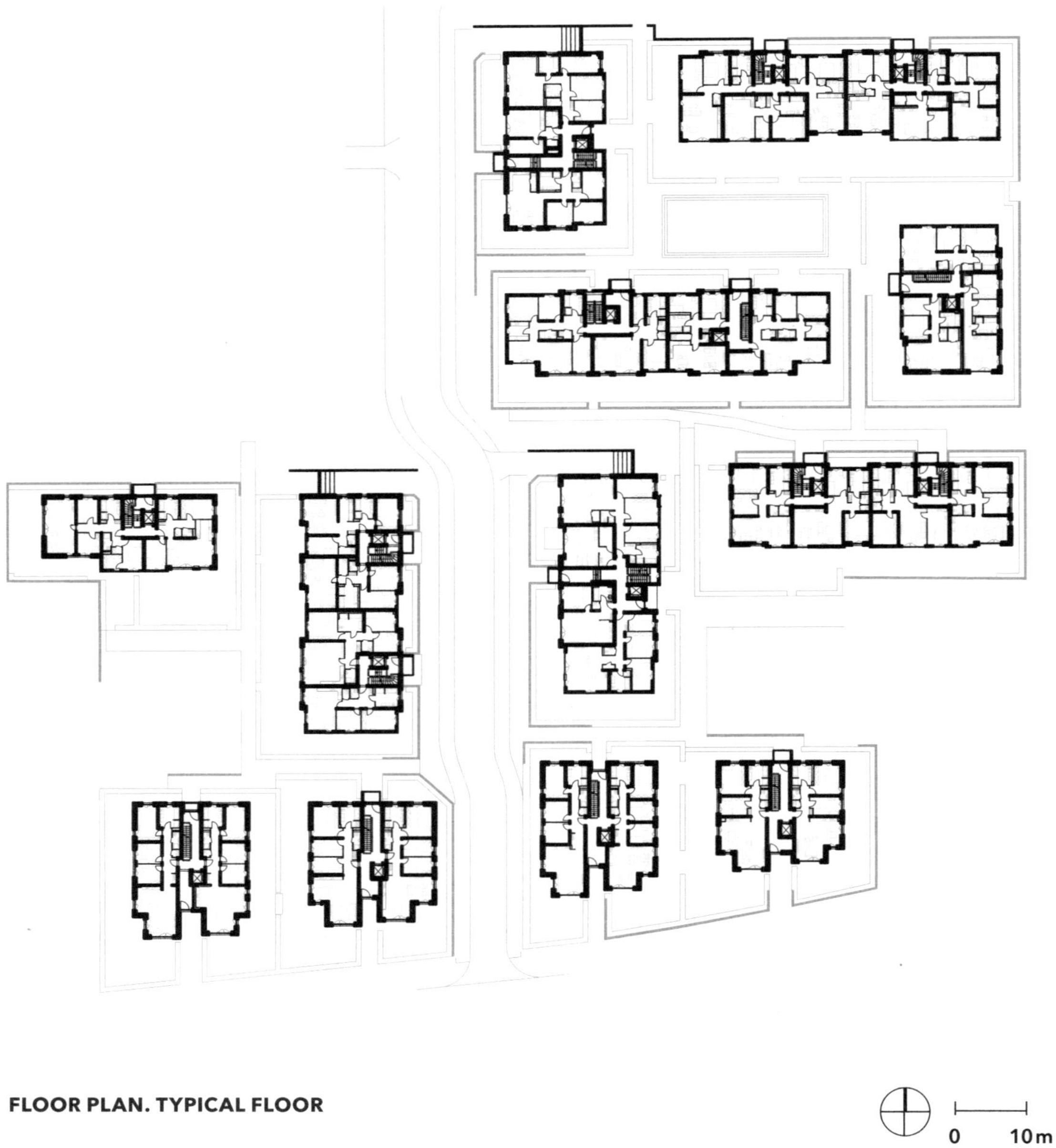

FLOOR PLAN. TYPICAL FLOOR

SÜDERFELD PARK, HAMBURG

ACKERSTRASSE 29, BERLIN

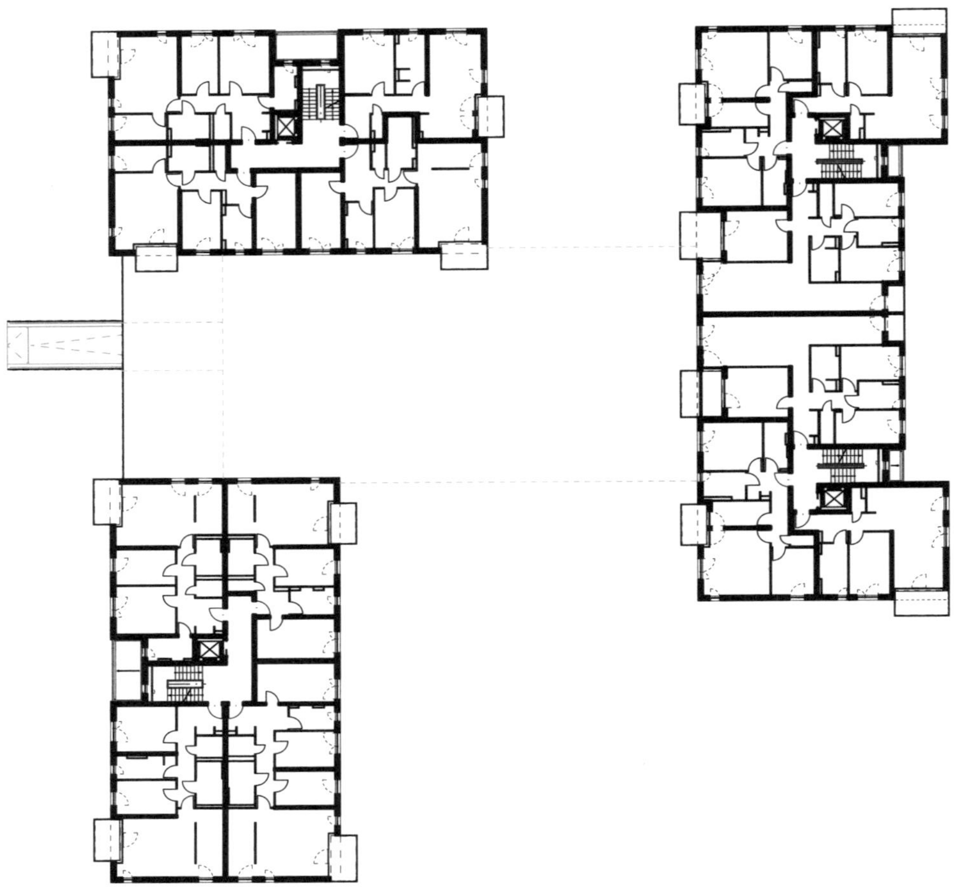

FLOOR PLAN. TYPICAL FLOOR

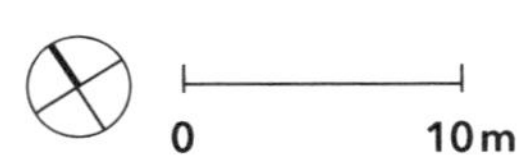

CLARA-ZETKIN-STRASSE, LUDWIGSFELDE

FINKENAU, FAMILY NEIGHBORHOOD, HAMBURG

At Finkenau a new family district has involved the construction of 'Eleven Houses' – a total of 11 buildings containing approximately 154 apartments for sale and rental. After taking second place in the design competition, TCHOBAN VOSS Architekten built two of the eleven houses.

INDEX

' RESIDENTIAL AND BUSINESS BUILDINGS, HOTELS, RETAIL SPACES, OFFICE COMPLEXES; ARCHITECTURE FOR LEISURE, EDUCATION, AND SOCIAL FUNCTIONS; CONVERSION PROJECTS AND REVITALIZATION OF EXISTING LISTED BUILDINGS: FOR THESE TYPES OF PROJECT WE HAVE ALWAYS PROVIDED A FULL RANGE OF ARCHI-TECTURAL SERVICES, FROM INTERIOR DESIGN TO GENERAL PLANNING.

TCHOBAN VOSS ARCHITEKTEN

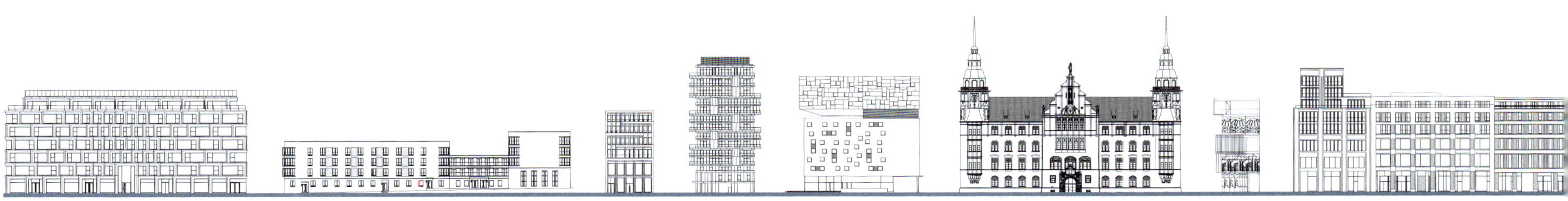

PROJECT ESSAYS

MUSEUM FOR ARCHITECTURAL DRAWING

Address: Christinenstraße 18a, 10119 Berlin
Client: Tchoban Foundation – Museum für Architekturzeichnung, Berlin
Gross floor area: 498 m²
Completion: May 2013
Architect: Sergei Tchoban, Sergey Kuznetsov / SPEECH, Moskau
Architectural design and construction management: TCHOBAN VOSS Architekten, Berlin
Project partner and project manager: Philipp Bauer, Ulrike Graefenhain
Team: Nadja Fedorova, Katja Fuks, Dirk Kollendt, Frederik-Sebastian Scholz

pp. 16 ff.

LANDGERICHT HALLE

Address: Hansering 13, 06108 Halle (Saale)
Client: Landesbetrieb Bau Sachsen-Anhalt, NL Süd
Gross floor area: 13,686 m²
Completion: December 2012
Architect: Alf M. Prasch
Associate partner: Jörg Rudloff
Project manager: Bettina Kempe-Gebert
Team: Jörn Ahlhelm, Susanne Bahr, Frank Helms, Verena Liebo, Christoph Schröter, Kay Wenzel, Holm Zink

pp. 26 ff.

NAUEN TOWN BATHS

Address: Karl-Thon-Straße 20a, 14641 Nauen
Client: Stadt Nauen, DLG Dienstleistungsgesellschaft Nauen mbH
Gross floor area: 630 m²
Completion: July 2017
Architect: Sergei Tchoban
Project manager: Jan Frechen
Team: Karsten Waldschmidt, Guido Kall, Jan Lisner, Stefan Petro, René Hoch, Azzurra Pippia, Michael Both

pp. 34 ff.

FEDERATION COMPLEX

Address: Presnenskaya Naberezhnaya 12, 123100 Moskau, Russland
Client: AEON Corporation
Gross floor area: 433,000 m²
Completion: Turm Ost: 2017 / Turm West: 2008
Conceptual authors: Peter Schweger, Sergei Tchoban
Architects: TCHOBAN VOSS Architekten, Berlin / SAA Schweger Architekten, Hamburg / SPEECH, Moskau
Project managers: Competition: TCHOBAN VOSS Architekten: Valeria Kashirina, Paul Olufs / ASP: Philipp Kahl, Tilman Kriesel
Architectural design: TCHOBAN VOSS Architekten: Matthias Lassen, Matthias Dahlmann, Lidia Rtiseva / SPEECH: Sergey Glubokin, Andrey Perlich
Team: TCHOBAN VOSS Architekten: Stefan Barme, Kirill Chaljawski, Kristian Dahlgard, Jörn Frenzel, Peter Galonska, Philipp Gubkin, Christoph Heimermann, Ilana Hofmann, Susanne Janitzky, Natalia von Krüchten, Anissa Landgraf, Ines Lehmann, Anna Linda-Kinder, Igor Markov, Anja Mattern, Tatjana Rabinovitch, Katja Redmann, Anna Sacharowa, Stefanie Seegerer, Steffen Thauer, Pavel Zemskov / SPEECH: Wladimir Chaljawski, Alexandra Glotova, Svetlana Shilova, Lubov Shirokova, Tatyana Zhokhova

pp. 40 ff.

HOUSING ON HOLZHALBINSEL

Address: Loggerweg, Gaffelschonerweg (Holzhalbinsel), 18055 Rostock
Client: WIRO Wohnen in Rostock, Wohnungsgesellschaft mbH, Rostock
Gross floor area: 20,820 m²
Completion: August 2018
Architect: Alf M. Prasch
Associate partner: Frank Focke

Project managers: Bernd Borgolte, Anja Dähne
Supervision of construction: Johannes Galandi
Team: Serhat Akdoganlar, Anja Dähne, Falko Holtz, Klaus Mehlhorn, Thomas Reich, Annika Suck

pp. 50 ff.

BOXHAGENER STRASSE

Address: Boxhagener Straße 79–82, 10245 Berlin
Client: BAUWERT Boxhagener Straße GmbH, Bad Kötzting
Gross floor area: 10,973 m²
Completion: October 2018
Architect: Sergei Tchoban
Project partner and project manager: Stephan Lohre
Team: Anja Schroth, Katharina Stranz, Katja Redmann, Virginie Mommens

pp. 58 ff.

RHINE-WAAL UNIVERSITY OF APPLIED SCIENCES

Address: Marie-Curie-Straße 1, 47533 Kleve
Client: Kreisverwaltung Kleve, Der Landrat, Wolfgang Spreen
Gross floor area: 41,470 m²
Completion: August 2012
Architect: Ekkehard Voss
Associate partner and project manager: Dierk Schafmeyer
Team: Pia Abraham, Denis Andre, Stefan Drese, Jan Hagen, Andreas Hensze, Anna Hoffmeister, Ulf Jensen, Perdita Jessen

pp. 66 ff.

SVEN WINGQUIST TEST CENTER

Address: Sven-Wingquist-Straße 6, 97424 Schweinfurt
Client: SKF GmbH, Schweinfurt
Gross floor area: 5828 m²
Completion: April 2017
Architect: Ekkehard Voss
Associate partner: Frank Focke
Project manager: Stephan Müller
Team: Annett Neitzel, Daniel Schnettka

pp. 74 ff.

REPORTS

MUSIC AND LIFESTYLE HOTEL NHOW

Address: Stralauer Allee 3, 10245 Berlin
Client: NDC Nippon Development Corporation, Berlin
Gross floor area: 21,463 m²
Completion: November 2010
Architect: Sergei Tchoban
Project partner and project manager: Axel Binder
Team: Kenan Ozan, Andrea Moritz, Natalia von Krüchten, Manuela Peth

pp. 84 ff.

COCA-COLA HQ

Address: Stralauer Allee 4, 10245 Berlin
Client: Hochtief Projektentwicklung GmbH, NL Berlin-Brandenburg
Gross floor area: 10,263 m²
Completion: April 2013
Architect: Sergei Tchoban
Project partner and project manager: Philipp Bauer, Axel Binder
Team: Christoph Heimermann, Anissa Landgraf, Kenan Ozan

pp. 84 ff.

THE WHITE

Address: Stralauer Allee 5, 10245 Berlin
Client: Wulff Hanseatische Bauträger GmbH, Hamburg
Gross floor area: 8572 m²
Completion: July 2016
Architect: Sergei Tchoban
Project partner: Philipp Bauer
Project managers: Philipp Bauer, Karsten Waldschmidt
Team: Anissa Landgraf, Priska-Magdalena Schwalke

pp. 84 ff.

BETHANIEN-HÖFE

Address: Martinistraße 41–49, 20251 Hamburg
Client: Bethanien Diakonissen-Stiftung, Frankfurt/Main
Gross floor area: 22,440 m²
Completion: August 2015
Architect: Ekkehard Voss
Associate partner: Stefan Niemöller
Project managers: Beate Schonlau, Christoph Niethammer
Team: Michael Both, Marion Mews, Annett Neitzel, Daniel Schnettka

pp. 118 ff.

FOCUS STORIES

NEUE SCHÖNHAUSER 15

Address: Neue Schönhauser Straße 15, 10178 Berlin
Client: Prime Development Property GmbH
Gross floor area: 2050 m²
Completion: April 2014
Architect: Sergei Tchoban
Associate partner: Frederik-Sebastian Scholz
Team: Anja Koch

pp. 100 f.

VOCATIONAL COLLEGE WITH THREE-PITCH SPORTS HALL

Address: Am Nierspark 35, 47608 Geldern
Client: Kreis Kleve
Gross floor area: approx. 15,620 m² / 2670 m²
Completion: August 2016
Architect: Ekkehard Voss
Associate partner: Dierk Schafmeyer
Project manager: Felix Hildebrand
Team: Jens Böttcher, Karolin Böttcher, Stephan Egert, Axel Neubauer, Annika Suck, Justine von Kossak, Mariella Kiourktsoglou

pp. 102 f.

ST. GEORG RUSSIAN MONASTERY CHURCH

Address: Götschendorf 33, 17268 Milmersdorf-Götschendorf
Client: The Berlin Diocese of the Russian Orthodox Church (Moscow Patriarchate)
Gross floor area: 358 m²
Completion: March 2017
Architect: Sergei Tchoban
Project partner: Philipp Bauer
Project managers: Dirk Kollendt, Karsten Waldschmidt, Simon Bange
Team: Katja Fuks, Natalia von Krüchten, Ramona Schwarzweller, Ingo Schwarzweller

pp. 104 f.

CHABAD LUBAWITSCH SYNAGOGUE

Address: Münstersche Str. 6, 10709 Berlin
Client: Chabad Lubawitsch Berlin e. V.
Gross floor area: 2050 m²
Completion: September 2007
Architect: Sergei Tchoban
Associate partner: Frederik-Sebastian Scholz
Team: Anja Schroth

pp. 106 f.

LIPPE BAD LÜNEN

Address: Konrad-Adenauer-Straße 28, 44534 Lünen
Client: Bädergesellschaft Lünen mbH
Gross floor area: 6500 m²
Completion: September 2011
Architect: Ekkehard Voss
Project manager: Andreas Hitz
Team: Maria Herbst, Marion Mews, Hajo Massel, Hoa Nguyen

pp. 108 f.

LIVING LEVELS

Address: Mühlenstraße 60, 10243 Berlin
Client: cic property & developement GmbH, Berlin
Gross floor area: 7800 m²
Completion: August 2015
Architect: Sergei Tchoban
Project partner and project manager: Philipp Bauer
Project manager: Karsten Waldschmidt
Team: Kenan Ozan, Christoph Heimermann, Anja Schroth, Stephan Luda-Scharping

pp. 110 f.

SCHENEFELDER HOLT

Address: Schenefelder Holt 135, 22589 Hamburg
Client: Bauverein der Elbgemeinden eG, Hamburg
Gross floor area: 8640 m²
Completion: May 2013
Architect: Ekkehard Voss
Project manager: Albert Feldkamp
Team: Frank Buken, Justine von Kossak, Annika Suck

pp. 112 f.

NEUER HÜHNERPOSTEN MICRO APARTMENTS

Address: Schultzweg 2, 20097 Hamburg
Client: Otto Wulff Projektentwicklung GmbH
Gross floor area: 16,938 m²
Completion: May 2016
Architect: Alf M. Prasch
Associate partner: Frank Focke
Project managers: Stefan Drese, Nils Höpken
Team: Jens Böttcher, Martin Hertel, Anke Kitel, Matthias Koch, Tomasz Kozaczek, Hajo Massel, Philipp Mogwitz, Axel Neubauer, Stefan Niemöller, Hoa Nguyen

pp. 114 f.

STUDENT ACCOMMODATION DRESDEN

Address: Holzhofgasse 1–5, 01099 Dresden
Client: GSA – Global Student Accommodation, Mainz
Gross floor area: 7502 m² / 1360 m² (underground)
Completion: May 2016
Architect: Alf M. Prasch
Associate partner: Jörg Rudloff
Project managers: Christoph Schröter, Frank Buken
Team: Christoph Schröter, Romy Kanitz, Harald Gatter, Matthias Korntheuer, Christina Ebisch

pp. 116 f.

FEATURE TOPIC

WORK ENVIRONMENTS

GLACIS-GALERIE

Address: Im Starkfeld 1-9, 89231 Neu-Ulm
Client: OfB & Procom Objekt Neu-Ulm GmbH & Co. KG
Gross floor area: 104,733 m²
Completion: March 2015
Architect: Ekkehard Voss
Associate partner and project manager: Dierk Schafmeyer
Project manager: Christoph Klüsserath
Team: Marcel Bender, Bernd Borgolte, Jens Böttcher, Susanne Born, Marie Carl, Stefan Drese, Sven Grützmann, Jan Hagen, Martin Hertel, Felix Hildebrand, Nils Höpken, Anna Hoffmeister, Ulf Jensen, Perdita Jessen, Stefan Kahn, Matthias Koch, Justine von Kossak, Tomasz Kozaczek, Hajo Massel, Jessica Mertens, Philipp Mogwitz, Stephan Müller, Alexander Off, Henrik Priebe, Constance von Rege, Thomas Sperfeldt, Annika Suck, Thorben Trapp, Gerhard von Wyscecki

p. 132

LP 12 MALL OF BERLIN

Address: Leipziger Platz 12-13 / Leipziger Straße 129-135 / Voßstraße 24-32, 34-35 / Wilhelmstraße 79-80, 10117 Berlin
Client: HGHI Holding GmbH, Berlin
Gross floor area: 210,000 m²
Completion: September 2014
Architect: Sergei Tchobanin work team with Pechtold Gesellschaft von Architekten mbH
Project partner: Stephan Lohre
Project managers: Ulrike Graefenhain, Frederik-Sebastian Scholz
Façade design: Valeria Kashirina
Team: Stefan Barme, Nadja Federova, Silvia Grischkat, Katja Gursch, René Hoch, Birgit Köder, Irena Ludwig, Elina Mihajlova, Vicky Moutzouri, Fabiana Pedretti, Manuela Peth, Katharina Stranz, Niina Trunova

pp. 132 f.

GROSSE BLEICHEN OFFICE AND BUSINESS BUILDING

Address: Große Bleichen 19, 20354 Hamburg
Client: Aachener Grundvermögen Kapitalverwaltungsgesellschaft mbH, Köln
Gross floor area: 6652 m²
Completion: December 2018
Architect: Ekkehard Voss
Project managers: Christoph Klüsserath, Perdita Jessen
Team: Serhat Akdoganlar, Michael Both, Karolin Böttcher, Jens Böttcher, Jan Kumbernuss, Mona Tausend

pp. 134 f.

TUCHFABRIK

Address: Friedrich-Olbricht-Damm 62, 13627 Berlin
Client: FOD Immobilien GmbH, Berlin
Gross floor area: 2860 m²
Completion: July 2016
Architect: Sergei Tchoban
Project manager: Pavel Zemskov
Façade design: Valeria Kashirina
Team: Silvia Grischkat, René Hoch, Evgenija Sulaberidze, Katja Fuks, Lev Chestakov

pp. 136 f.

VOLKSWOHL BUND VERSICHERUNGEN, DORTMUND

Address: Südwall 37-41, 44137 Dortmund
Client: Volkswohl Bund Versicherungen
Gross floor area: 30,644 m²
Completion: December 2010
Architect: Ekkehard Voss
Associate partners: Stefan Niemöller, Christoph Klüsserath
Project managers: Albert Feldkamp, Stephan Müller
Team: Michael Both, Phillip Mogwitz, Marion Mews, Ole Kelting, Annika Suck, Justine v. Kossak, Stephanie Herholz, Hajo Massel, Hoa Nguyen, Tomasz Kozaczek

pp. 138 f.

KVS SACHSEN

Address: Marschnerstraße 37, 01307 Dresden
Client: Zusatzversorgungskasse des Kommunalen Versorgungsverbandes Sachsen
Gross floor area: 5021 m²
Completion: May 2015
Architect: Alf M. Prasch
Associate partner: Jörg Rudloff
Project manager: Bettina Kempe
Team: Kay Wenzel, Holm Zink

pp. 140 f.

SCHLOSS SONNENSTEIN

Address: Schloss Sonnenstein, 01796 Pirna
Client: Landratsamt Sächsische Schweiz-Osterzgebirge
Gross floor area: 17,875 m² (buildings) / 7587 m² (car park)
Completion: December 2011
Architect: Alf M. Prasch
Associate partner and project manager: Jörg Rudloff
Project manager: Holm Dietrich
Team: Harald Getter, Frank Helms, Verena Liebo

pp. 148 f.

GROSSE HAMBURGER STRASSE

Address: Große Hamburger Straße 17, 10178 Berlin
Client: Schauder & Shani GmbH, Berlin
Gross floor area: 2338 m²
Completion: October 2010
Architect: Sergei Tchoban
Associate partner: Frederik-Sebastian Scholz
Team: Anja Koch, Christian Barwe

pp. 152 f.

DEVELOPMENT

MAGDEBURG REGIONAL COURT HOUSE

Address: Halberstädter Straße 8, 39112 Magdeburg
Client: Bau- und Liegenschaftsmanagement Sachsen-Anhalt (BLSA)
Gross floor area: 19,635 m²
Completion: April 2020
Architect: Ekkehard Voss
Associate partner: Jörg Rudloff
Project manager: Bettina Kempe-Gebert
Team: Susanne Bahr, Laura Feldmann, Tobias Frisch, Jörg Rathmann, Stefan Schönefuss, Gabi Vogt

pp. 146 f.

ERNST-REUTER-HAUS

Address: Straße des 17. Juni 110–114, 10623 Berlin
Client: Cenda Invest AG, Berlin
Gross floor area: 25,596 m²
Completion: August 2011
Architect: Sergei Tchoban
Project partner and project manager: Philipp Bauer
Team: René Hoch, Anissa Landgraf, Christian Strauß, Dirk Kollendt, Antje Kalus

pp. 150 f.

HOTELS

HOTELS AT HAUPTBAHNHOF

Address: Invalidenstraße / Heidestraße, Europaplatz, 10557 Berlin
Client: S & R Beteiligungs GmbH & Co, Berlin
Gross floor area: 22,040 m²
Completion: August 2015
Architect: Sergei Tchoban
Project partner and project manager: Axel Binder
Team: Patrick Dannehl, Virginie Mommens, Andrea Moritz, Andreas Lenz

pp. 156 f.

HOTEL AM NORDKOPF

Address: Willy-Brandt-Platz, 38440 Wolfsburg
Client: GBI AG
Gross floor area: 10,450 m²
Completion: May 2015
Architect: Sergei Tchoban
Project partner and project manager: Axel Binder
Team: Andreas Lenz, Andrea Moritz

pp. 158 f.

MEININGER HOTEL AT POSTBAHNHOF

Address: Am Postbahnhof 4, 10243 Berlin
Client: NDC Nippon Development Corporation
Gross floor area: 7375 m²
Completion: 2017
Architect: Sergei Tchoban
Project partner: Philipp Bauer
Project manager: Dirk Kollendt
Team: Achim Linde, Hanna Bulanava, Alina Molina

pp. 160 f.

MELIÁ HOTEL DÜSSELDORF

Address: Inselstraße 2, 40479 Düsseldorf
Client: GII Grundbesitz Investitionsgesellschaft mbH & Co. KG, Hamburg
Gross floor area: 16,183 m²
Completion: February 2009
Architect: Alf M. Prasch
Associate partner and project manager: Frank Focke
Team: Anja Dähne, Bernd Borgolte, Ralf Grigoleit

pp. 162 f.

TITANIC HOTEL

Address: Chausseestraße 30, 10115 Berlin
Client: Moonday Projektentwicklungsgesellschaft GmbH, Berlin
Gross floor area: 33,606 m²
Completion: July 2015
Architect: Sergei Tchoban
Associate partner: Frederik-Sebastian Scholz
Project manager: Holm Dietrich
Team: Clemens Döhler, Silvia Grischkat, Frank Helms, Christoph Schröter

pp. 164 f.

HOUSING

STUDENT RESIDENCE ON BRIENER STRASSE

Address: Briener Straße 45, 47533 Kleve
Client: Studentenwerk Düsseldorf
Gross floor area: 4787 m²
Completion: February 2013
Architect: Ekkehard Voss
Associate partner and project manager: Dierk Schafmeyer
Team: Anna Hoffmeister, Ulf Jensen

p. 169

SÜDERFELD PARK

Address: Süderfeldstraße 24–30 / Heinrich-Kock-Weg 1–18, 22529 Hamburg
Client: J. H. Gustav Burmeister GmbH & Co. KG, Hamburg
Gross floor area: 20,500 m²
Completion: April 2018
Architect: Ekkehard Voss
Associate partner: Stefan Niemöller
Project managers: Beate Schonlau, Andreas Hitz
Team: Steffen Böhm, Michael Both, Maria Herbst, Sarah Köhler, Marion Mews, Annett Neitzel

pp. 170 f.

ACKERSTRASSE 29

Address: Ackerstraße 29, 10115 Berlin
Client: Acker 28 Projektgesellschaft GmbH & Co KG
Gross floor area: 3125 m²
Completion: September 2016
Architect: Sergei Tchoban
Project partner: Philipp Bauer, Karsten Waldschmidt
Project manager: Philipp Bauer
Team: Kenan Ozan, Katja Fuks, Natalia von Kruechten, Anissa Landgraf

pp. 172 f.

CLARA-ZETKIN-STRASSE

Address: Lise-Meitner-Str. / Clara-Zetkin-Str., 14974 Ludwigsfelde
Client: Ludwigsfelder Wohnungsgenossenschaft eG
Gross floor area: 8773 m²
Completion: September 2018
Architect: Ekkehard Voss
Associate partner: Jörg Rudloff
Project manager: Jan Klömich
Team: Magdalena Bolavec, Harald Gatter, Frank Helms, Karsten Kuhn, Julya Wustrau, Holm Zink

pp. 174 f.

FAMILY QUARTER FINKENAU (2 OF 11 HOUSES)

Address: Finkenau 19–23 / Dorothea-Bernstein-Weg 1–15, 22081 Hamburg
Client: Günther Franke Gruber Bauherren GmbH
Gross floor area: 3760 m² (Houses 1+2) / 18,000 m² (in total)
Completion: December 2014
Architect: Ekkehard Voss
Project manager: Christoph Niethammer
Team: Stephan Egert, Jan Hagen, Marina Hoffmann, Tomasz Kozaczek, Hajo Massel, Marion Mews, Philipp Mogwitz, Annett Neitzel, Axel Neubauer, Hoa Nguyen

p. 176

TEAM

More than 150 employees in all fields of architecture are what make us strong. Our in-house services include model-making, graphic design, and 3D-visualization. Where necessary, we can call upon an international network of qualified engineers and specialists. We respond to the changes of our time with curiosity and keep abreast of the latest developments through continuous training and innovative technology.

HAMBURG

MANAGING PARTNER
Voss, Ekkehard

ASSOCIATE PARTNER
Focke, Frank
Klüsserath, Christoph
Schafmeyer, Dierk
Commercial Director, Dipl.-Wirtschaftsingenieur (FH), ppa. Jörg Schulte

TEAM
Akdoganlar, Serhat
Berardi, Dario
Berg, Catrin
Böhm, Steffen
Born, Susanne
Both, Michael
Böttcher, Karolin
Carl, Marie
Clasen, Martina
Dähne, Anja
Dieseldorff, Alessandra
Egert, Stephan
Feldkamp, Albert
Fröse, David
Galandi, Johannes
Grigoleit, Ralf
Gühlke, Julya
Hagen, Jan
Hahn, Werner
Haller, Claudia
Herbst, Maria
Hildebrand, Felix
Hitz, Andreas
Hohaus, Magdalena
Höpken, Nils
Huck, Peter
Ihm, Georg
Jessen, Perdita
Julià-Xercavins, Carla
Kiourktsoglou, Maria
Klappoth, Daniela
Knopp, Adrian
Koch, Mathias
Kozaczek, Tomasz
Kuhn, Felix
Kunz, Timo
Linke, Larissa
Löbig, Christopher
Loss, Alexander
Massel, Hajo
Meyer, Paul
Mogwitz, Philipp
Müller, Stephan
Neitzel, Annett
Neubauer, Axel
Neuberger, Torsten
Nguyen, Hoa
Off, Alexander
Otte, Ramon
Ovechkin, Sergey
Papa, Pasqualina
Petereit, Daniel
Rickling, Christiane
Schierloh, Jürgen
Schnettka, Daniel
Schonlau, Beate
Siebke, Kai
Sonntag, Steffen
Sperfeldt, Thomas
Steinhorst, Iris
Suck, Annika
Walch, Aude
Willers, Yara Sophie
Wünscher, Julia

BERLIN

MANAGING PARTNER
Tchoban, Sergei

PARTNER | ASSOCIATE PARTNER
Bauer, Philipp
Binder, Axel
Krebes, Martin
Lohre, Stephan
Scholz, Frederik Sebastian

TEAM
Andreeva-Florian, Andreyana
Angelstorf, Julia
Ballheimer, Niina
Bange, Simon
Beese, Johannes
Beliakova, Tatiana
Besana, Massimo
Beyer, Clemens
Bulanava, Hanna
Chestakov, Lev
Dorner, Franziska
Durán Calero, Juan
Fedorova, Nadejda
Fontana, Giorgia
Frechen, Jan
Fuks, Katja
Goldberg, Polina
Gradinarova, Liza
Graefenhain, Ulrike
Hoch, René
Kapustina, Anastasia
Kashirina, Valeria
Klähn, Jennifer
Kleinschumacher, Merle
Köder, Birgit
Kollendt, Dirk
Landgraf, Anissa
Lee, Woo-Chung
Lennertz, Charlotte
Llinares Ruiz, Marc
Lohse, Theresa
Meshkova, Svetlana
Mizzon, Angelo
Mjavanadze, Giorgi
Molina, Alina
Mommens, Virginie
Moritz, Andrea
Mylopoulou, Aristea
O'Gorman, Eimear
Ozan, Kenan
Pagenstecher, Mareike
Pedretti, Fabiana
Peth, Manuela
Petricic, Dennis
Petro, Stefan
Pippia, Azzurra
Plotkina, Polina
Rabitsch, Andrej
Redmann, Katja
Ricci, Daniele
Schreiber, Dean
Schroth, Anja
Schwarzweller, Ingo
Schwarzweller, Ramona
Sezdi, Burhan
Stranz, Katharina
Sulaberidze, Evgenia
Trahorsch, Carolin
van Ost, Soeren
von Krüchten, Natalia
Wendland, Nancy
Zaranis, Fotios Seigia
Zemskov, Pavel

DRESDEN

ASSOCIATE PARTNER
Rudloff, Jörg

TEAM
Ahrendt, Dennis
Bauriegel, Wolfgang
Bayer, Philipp
Bolavec, Magdalena
Dietrich, Holm
Drechsler, Stefan
Farrow, Anke
Feldmann, Laura
Frisch, Tobias
Gatter, Harald
Helms, Frank
Hofmann, Susanne
Kempe-Gebert, Bettina
Klömich, Jan
Liebo, Verena
Rathmann, Jörg
Schröter, Christoph
Specht, Julia
Vázquez Enriquez, Joaquin
Voigt, Gabriele
Will, Laura
Wyzisk, Burkhard
Zink, Holm

BIOGRAPHIES

SERGEI TCHOBAN
ASSOCIATION OF GERMAN ARCHITECTS

Sergei Tchoban (born in 1962) is an internationally active architect. He is a managing partner in TCHOBAN VOSS Architekten, with responsibility for the firm's office in Berlin.

After studying at the Academy of Arts in Saint Petersburg, Sergei worked as a freelance architect in Russia. In 1992 he started working for Nietz Prasch Sigl Architekten in Hamburg, becoming a partner in the firm in 1995 and then taking charge of its office in Berlin in 1996. Since 2017 Sergei Tchoban and Ekkehard Voss have headed the firm under its new name of TCHOBAN VOSS Architekten.

Buildings and building ensembles by Sergei Tchoban have won him international recognition. His projects range from hotel, office, and residential buildings through mixed-use ensembles to modernization of existing buildings. Since 1992 Sergei Tchoban has been a member of the American Society of Architectural Illustrators (ASAI); his drawings have been shown at numerous museums and galleries and can be found in private and public collections, including in those belonging to the Architectural Archive at the Academy of Arts in Berlin and the Victoria & Albert Museum in London.

In 2018 Sergei Tchoban was awarded the European Prize for Architecture by the Chicago Athenaeum Museum of Architecture and Design.

EKKEHARD VOSS
ASSOCIATION OF GERMAN ARCHITECTS

Ekkehard Voss (born in 1963) practises as an architect in Germany. He is a managing partner at TCHOBAN VOSS Architekten, with responsibility for the firm's offices in Hamburg and Dresden.

After graduating from RWTH Aachen and his first years of architectural practice in Düsseldorf, in 1992 he settled in Hamburg, where he worked tor Nietz Prasch Sigl Architekten, the precursor of TCHOBAN VOSS Architekten. He became a partner in the firm, alongside Sergei Tchoban, in 1995. Since 2017 the two long-term partners head the firm under its new name, TCHOBAN VOSS Architekten.

Numerous highly praised buildings and ensembles have been built to designs by Ekkehard Voss. The fields in which he specializes are housing, educational buildings, office and retail space, and development of existing buildings. Many of these projects have been built in collaboration with public clients.

Ekkehard Voss represents TCHOBAN VOSS Architekten as a member of EAN (European Architects Network).

AWARDS

AWARDS (2014–18, SELECTION)

2018 **European Prize for Architecture 2018 |** Sergei Tchoban

2018 **The International Architecture Award 2018 |** Sven Wingquist Test Center, Schweinfurt

2018 **BDA Hamburg Architektur Preis | 3. prize:** Große Bleichen office and business building, Hamburg

2018 **The Plan | Honorable Mention:** Nauen Town Baths

2017 **The International Architecture Award 2017 |** Landgericht Halle

2017 **Iconic Awards | Winner:** Tuchfabrik, Coca-Cola HQ, Berlin

2017 **German Design Award | Special Mention in Architecture:** Coca-Cola HQ, Hotels at Hauptbahnhof, Berlin

2017 **German Design Award | Special Mention in Architecture:** Hotels at Hauptbahnhof Berlin

2016 **Brillux Jubiläums-Fassadenpreis | 1. prize:** Schenefelder Holt, Hamburg

2016 **Iconic Awards | Winner in Public Architecture:** Bethanien-Höfe, Hamburg

2016 **FIABCI Prix d'Excellence | Official Selection 2016:** Living Levels, Berlin

2015 **Europe Property Awards Architecture | Best Public Service Architecture Germany:** Museum for Architectural Drawing, Berlin

2015 **The International Architecture Award 2015 |** Hotel am Nordkopf, Wolfsburg

2015 **Deutscher Lichtdesign-Preis | Award in Category Museums:** Museum for Architectural Drawing, Berlin

2014 **Heinze ArchitektenAWARD 2015 | Winner of Faszination Nichtwohnbau:** Museum for Architectural Drawing, Berlin

2014 **German Design Award | Winner in Excellent Communications Design, Architecture and Urban Design:** Museum for Architectural Drawing, Berlin

2014 **The International Architecture Award 2014 |** Museum for Architectural Drawing, Berlin

2014 **DAM Preis für Architektur | Die besten 24 Bauten in und aus Deutschland:** Museum for Architectural Drawing, Berlin

2014 **Bau des Jahres, german-architects.com | 2. prize:** Museum for Architectural Drawing, Berlin

NOMINATION (2014–18, SELECTION)

2018 **DAM Preis für Architektur 2018 | Nomination:** Federation Complex, Moscow, The White, Berlin

2018 **WAF Award | Finalist:** Sven Wingquist Test Center, Schweinfurt

2018 **Architizer A+ Awards | Finalist:** Sven Wingquist Test Center, Schweinfurt

2017 **LEAF awards | Shortlist:** The White, Berlin

2017 **WAF Awards | Shortlist:** Tuchfabrik, Ackerstraße 29, Berlin, St. Georg Russian Monastery Church, Götschendorf

2017 **Wienerberger Brick Award | Nominierung:** St. Georg Russian Monastery Church, Götschendorf

2017 **The Plan | Finalist:** Living Levels, Berlin

2017 **DAM Preis für Architektur 2017 | Nomination:** Living Levels, Berlin

2016 **WAF Award | Shortlist:** Living Levels, Berlin

2016 **DAM Internationaler Hochhauspreis | Nomination:** Federation Complex, Moscow

2015 **LEAF awards | Shortlist:** LP 12 Mall of Berlin

2015 **AZ Awards 2015 | Finalist: Architecture < 1000 sqm:** Museum for Architectural Drawing, Berlin

2014 **MiesArch 2015 | Nomination:** Museum for Architectural Drawing, Berlin

2014 **Archmarathon 2014 | Shortlist:** Museum for Architectural Drawing, Berlin

2014 **Architizer A+ Awards | Special Mention: Museums:** Museum for Architectural Drawing, Berlin

2014 **AIT Award | Special Mention:** Museum für Architekturzeichnung, Berlin

AUTHORS

TIM BERGE studied architecture at Berlin University of the Arts. After several years as a practising architect, he began working as a journalist, including for BauNetz and Dear Magazin, and as a writer and communications strategist with a focus on architecture, design, and urban planning.

FRANZISKA EIDNER is a co-founder of EINSATEAM – a theme-oriented communications agency based in Berlin. A graduate of courses in journalism and cultural studies, Franziska is interested in contexts involving architecture, design, and urban planning. She is managing editor of Bauhaus magazine and is a freelance author and publisher.

POLINA GOLDBERG studied urban planning at Berlin Institute of Technology (TU) Berlin and Institut Français d'Urbanisme in Paris. After graduating, she worked on the editorial board of BauNetz, writing on numerous themes at the interface between architecture and art. She has headed the press and PR department at TCHOBAN VOSS Architekten since 2015.

CHRISTINA GRÄWE is an architect who works as a freelance journalist and publicist for various specialist media. She is a co-publisher of Deutsches Architektur Jahrbuch (German Architecture Annual) and the annual Architekturführer Deutschland. As a partner of kuratorenwerkstatt Förster Gräwe Winkelmann, she has organized numerous exhibitions, especially for DAM (the German Architecture Museum).

JASMIN JOUHAR is a freelance author and editor. She regularly publishes on subjects relating to design and architecture in various German-language newspapers, publications, and specialist media, including in Frankfurter Allgemeine Sonntagszeitung, Ideat, Häuser, AIT and BauNetz.

JEANNETTE MERKER is a co-founder of EINSATEAM. After studying architecture and urban planning, she started specializing in communication at the interface between these two disciplines. In this context she regularly devises and realizes publications and exhibitions. In the period 2009-2015 she worked as a research assistant at the Department of Architectural Communication at Karlsruhe Institute of Technology.

LUISE RELLENSMANN is a freelance architecture journalist, focusing on conservation of listed buildings and on development of existing ones. In 2015–2018 she was a member of the board of the German National Committee of the International Council on Monuments and Sites (ICOMOS). Since April 2017 she has been pursuing a doctoral degree at the Department of Conservation of Monuments at Brandenburg University of Technology (BTU) Cottbus-Senftenberg.

AFTERWORD AND THANK YOU

This third book about TCHOBAN VOSS Architekten is an opportunity for us to attempt once again an architectural assessment of our daily creative work – work which we understand as an expression of architectural culture over the course of time. For us, as an architectural partnership, this publication is a mirror which provides both a critical view of our work and a motivation for future projects.

Our thanks go especially to EINSATEAM – namely to Franziska Eidner and Jeanette Merker, who have taken a fresh and knowledgeable approach to our firm's focal themes while placing TCHOBAN VOSS Achitekten in the social and architectonic context of our time. With their purposeful guidance and judicious support they have played a big part in the creation of this book; working together on this joint project has brought joy to all.

Judith Keller of EINSATEAM, who was responsible for the graphic design, has tackled her task with great patience and empathy for our wishes and ideas on presenting the buildings and projects. Her creative skill has born fruit in a presentation that is clear and appropriate to the architecture.

Our special thanks go to all participating authors and photographers; their texts and photographs are crucial for how our firm and work are seen.

Management and coordination of this book project, in collaboration with JOVIS Verlag, was handled in-house by Valeria Kashirina, Polina Goldberg, Lev Chestakov (Berlin) and Axel Neubauer (Hamburg). We would like to pay tribute to their passion for writing about architecture, together with that of all other participants who have contributed in word and deed to the success of this book.

Crucial for the diversity and architectural depth of high-quality buildings is the untiring commitment of our highly-motivated employees at our offices in Hamburg, Berlin, and Dresden. Under the leadership of our associated partners and project partners, they combine creative aspiration with professional passion, ensuring that together we produce high-quality architecture for ourselves and our clients.

Our sincere thanks to all of you.

Sergei Tchoban and Ekkehard Voss

IMPRINT

CREDITS

Lev Chestakov: 12, 13, 35–37, 39, 104, 105, 186
Dmitry Chistoprudov: 41, 45–46, 49
Christian Gahl: 150, 151
Claus Graubner: 10 t., 100, 101, 159
Roland Halbe: 18, 19, 23, 25, 59–63, 65, 110, 111, 153
Sven Heering: 149
Werner Huthmacher: 10 b. r., 94, 96, 136, 137, 172, 173
Julia Jungfer: 106, 107
Hans Jürgen Landes: 50, 53, 55–57, 66–68, 71, 73, 75–79, 81–83, 102, 103, 109, 139, 169
George Messaritakis: 17, 20–22
Meliá Düsseldorf: 163
Michael Moser: 27–29, 31–33, 116, 117, 140, 141, 145, 146, 175
Aleksey Naroditsky: 43, 47
Axel Neubauer: 6, 11, 126
Ernst Reinsch: 108
Adrian Schulz: 133
Jöchen Stüber: 176
Daniel Sumesgutner: 112–115, 125, 171
Holger Talinski: 9, 84, 85, 87–93, 95, 97, 118, 119, 121–124, 127, 128
Martin Tervoort: 156, 157, 160, 161, 164, 165
Markus Tollhopf: 135
TCHOBAN VOSS Architekten: 10 b. l.

Publishing editors:
Sergei Tchoban and Ekkehard Voss |
TCHOBAN VOSS Architekten

Concept:
Franziska Eidner and Jeannette Merker | EINSATEAM
together with Valeria Kashirina

Editorial board:
Valeria Kashirina, Axel Neubauer, Polina Goldberg,
Lev Chestakov | TCHOBAN VOSS Architekten
Franziska Eidner, Jeannette Merker | EINSATEAM

Translation: John Nicolson

Design and typesetting: Judith Keller | EINSATEAM
Lithograph: Simon Adrian
Printed in the European Union

Bibliographic information published by the Deutsche Nationalbibliothek. The Deutsche Nationalbibliothek lists this publication in the Deutsche Nationalbibliografie; detailed bibliographic data are available on the Internet at http://dnb.d-nb.de

jovis Verlag GmbH
Kurfürstenstraße 15/16
10785 Berlin

www.jovis.de

jovis books are available worldwide in select bookstores. Please contact your nearest bookseller or visit www.jovis.de for information concerning your local distribution.

ISBN 978-3-86859-577-2